PUNCTUATION

BY

Joy Cotruzzola

Sapiens Press
a division of Joy Inc.
Albuquerque, NM

Sapiens Press
a division of Joy Inc.
2430 Juan Tabo, N.E.
Suite 256
Albuquerque, NM 87112

Library of Congress Cataloging in Publication Data

ISBN: 0-945904-04-5

Printed in the United States of America

9 8 7 6 5 4 3 2 1

CONTENTS

FOREWORD

As an old, old hand at teaching English, including everything from elementary grammar in high school to being on dissertation committees for graduate students, I applaud Joy Cotruzzola for turning out such a book as this. It is solid, readable, sound. She manages to cover every possible problem that a writer might run into in punctuating his/her work. But she does not tell you to write your article or essay or book and then look in her book to find out how to go back and punctuate your stuff. Punctuation does not stand that low in her regard. It is not some unimportant detail that can be left to a secretary or an editor. What you learn from this book about punctuation will serve you only when you have grasped the structure of sentences, have comprehended a large part of functional English grammar. I am pleased to note that she does not shy away from diagramming sentences. Every sample sentence is diagrammed. You have to keep your hold on the subject, the predicate, the kinds of sentences, clauses, phrases. You are given the material by which to understand what you are doing. You get away from guesswork in punctuation.

If I knew how to give the book a firmer or more enthusiastic endorsement, I would do so. I have not looked into an English grammar or a college freshman English handbook or the style book of the Modern Language Association in many years. I don't know whether the author is up-to-date in her pedagogy or not. I don't care. I have heard rumors in the last thirty years or so that a teacher is wasting his/her time and the students' time in trying to teach sentence diagramming, or the names of the parts of speech, or such technical terms as *dependent clause, adverbial modifier, conjunctive adverb*, and so on. If that is the official doctrine that has been prevailing, then I consider it to be nonsense. I am happy that Joy has tossed it out the window. What kind of an artisan is it that doesn't know the names of his tools? What kind of a piano student are you if you haven't worked through some Czerny exercises. (Exclude the geniuses if you wish. They can always find their own way.)

I now wish to take the liberty of adding a few random comments that might lead the reader of this book to understand a little better what a wonderful and flexible thing language is. No group of school teachers ever sat down and invented a language, its vocabulary, its spelling or words, the devices by which it communicates meaning. How language or speech ever got started is one of the great mysteries of life. Scholars have given up trying to explain it. But language was *oral* for a long time before it ever became written. Early language, therefore, built what we call punctuation right into the ways in which the words communicated. So we will always understand and use language better if we listen to it, if we hear the pauses, the length of the pauses, the changes in the pitch level; we are even helped to understand the speaker's intention if we can see his facial expressions and watch his body language.

I recommend, therefore, that when you are reading the sample sentences you read them aloud. The speed-readers will say no-no to this; but you can say no-no to them when you are trying to learn your basics. The experts say, or used to say, "Don't move your lips when you read; that just slows you down." I have only "anecdotal" evidence against this. My grandfather, who was born in 1846 and who never went beyond the sixth grade (because there was no grade higher than that within a hunderd miles of where he grew up) was what I call a lip-reader. He formed the words on his lips in a kind of whisper that I could hear all across the room. He taught me to read. I had to unlearn forming the words with my lips. But from those early days on through the long struggle to get a Ph.D. degree in English literature, I believe I have *heard in my mind's eye* almost every word I have read. (Don't tell me I have pulled off a mixed metaphor. I send a visual message to my brain. That message gets mysteriously metamorphosed into speech, into oral material. My lips don't move and my uvula doesn't wiggle—at least not often. I hear in my mind's eye. Let me admit that the phrase "mind's eye" was William Shakespeare's, but Shakespeare owns no copyrights.)

I repeat. When you are studying the author's excellent examples—they are often amusing—read them aloud. See if you don't almost *hear* where that pause is to go.

Also, when you come to an explanation—and there are many of them—and you don't quite understand, read the explanation at least twice, and then read it aloud at least once, and then go to the example and read it aloud. There is a very important cognitive principle here. There is a sequence: explanation to sample to rule, but in what order I don't know. But I do know that just looking up the rule is a primitive way to operate. If you will take the pains to go through the *process* that leads to the rule, you won't have to look up the rule again. You will have made something yours.

Punctuation isn't just rules. Punctuation is thinking straight.

Dudley Wynn, *Professor Emeritus of English, Dean Emeritus of Arts and Sciences, University of New Mexico, Dean Emeritus of General Honors*
Albuquerque, New Mexico
April 16, 1988

The first section of PUNCTUATION defines a number of symbols that you need to understand. They are simply written symbols which provide signals for every reader. Such written symbols are the road signs an author can use to direct a reader to the intended meaning. In fact, everything any writer does with mechanical English signs should be intended to help the reader understand the author's intent.

The second group of definitions concerns syntax. You need to understand the units that make up sentences. Also, the types of sentences that can be written need to be learned because varying your sentence types can prevent your writing from becoming boring to a reader.

After the mechanical signals and word units are defined, we will look at how a writer uses punctuation and capitalization to make his writing clearer and more meaningful. In other words, we will examine how the symbols actually function within writing.

While you are studying the mechanical signals, you will also be learning about syntax—the way in which words are put together to form expressive units. Although the word *syntax* may be unfamiliar, you have been using meaningful syntax since you began to speak. When you were just a baby, you learned to select the most expressive words in English—the nouns and verbs. Then you learned to combine all sorts of words into even more expressive units. You learned to speak in phrases, clauses, and sentences and express yourself more precisely. And that is what syntax is all about: how words are combined into larger units that say more.

Syntax is not the only thing you learned about English long before any teacher or book started telling you about the more formal aspects of English. You also learned the oral signals which make your language more expressive. Most of the mechanical signals an author uses are intended to make writing sound like speech. Therefore, since you have been using the signals in your oral language, you should not have too much trouble learning the most effective ways of using the written signals. Once you have learned what each mechanical signal does, almost everything you have to do with written symbols can be based upon the way you use pauses, stops, raised voice, or whatever in your oral speech. You may even increase the effectiveness of your oral language through your study of mechanical signals.

After you have studied PUNCTUATION for a short time, you will realize that all of the written symbols we use simply provide reading signals and additional information. They are the quickest, simplest means of aiding a reader to understand what you write while providing additional information without additional words. Fortunately, everything you need to learn about punctuation and capitalization is logical; it just makes sense when you look at how these signals work with words and groups of words.

Syntax is logical because it is based upon the way we effectively speak. If there were one type of syntax for speech and another for writing, we would probably have a great deal of difficulty writing. However, everything any writer should do is based upon effective communication, and almost all of our communication is based upon speech.

Although you probably will be able to see the logic of English mechanics and the usefulness of the signals by the end of the section directly concerning syntax, all of the ways to use mechanical signals may not be clear. That is why the next section of rules is included. The brief guide to using each signal may be useful in clearing up any confusion or lack of understanding.

The last part of PUNCTUATION is devoted to avoiding punctuation and capitalization errors. It also shows some ways that punctuation rules may be broken. As we said at the beginning of this introduction, all of the mechanical things a writer should do are just intended to get his meaning across to the reader. Occasionally breaking punctuation rules can help a writer show his meaning more clearly to a reader. If you will compare the examples in the "Errors that Lead to Poor Reading" with "Broken Rules for More Meaning," you will be able to see that punctuation is somewhat flexible.

Once you understand why and how punctuation is useful, you may occasionally want to ignore a punctuation rule, particularly in your fiction. However, if you truly understand how English mechanics work, you will use standard punctuation and capitalization almost all of the time. You will use all of the years and years of study that other people have done to determine how best to use mechanics to convey whatever you want to say.

Please remember, if anything is worth the time it takes you to write it, it should be worth saying in a manner that your reader can easily read and comprehend your meaning. English mechanics is simply intended to help you or any writer get the meaning across to a reader. The reason English mechanics is logical is that everything is based upon giving signals that help them make sense out of written words.

Finally, don't feel peculiar if you fail to understand everything at first. If you did not know much of this information before, it will take a little time for everything to make sense. Also, people best learn the same information through different approaches. You may find the discussion of mechanics and syntax most helpful. Others may find the brief summary of rules most helpful. Concentrate on whichever approach makes the most sense to you. It will help you understand the information in the other sections.

STUDY HINTS

Quickly read through all of PUNCTUATION. This will help you discover which presentation makes the most sense to you. You will also become familiar with the contents.

During the second reading of PUNCTUATION, which should be more thorough:

1. Underline what you consider to be the most important parts.
2. Put a question mark beside anything that you do not understand.
3. Compare the information in the section concerning mechanics and syntax with the information in the "Summary of Rules."
4. Carefully read all sentences in the "examples" sections. If you do not understand why something is punctuated the way it is, compare that example to the examples you understand in the same part of the discussion.

PUNCTUATION SYMBOLS

1. **Apostrophe (')**: used for the possessive case or to show omission of letters, as in contraction.

2. **Comma (,)**: used to separate words, phrases, and clauses from other sentence parts.

3. **Colon (:)**: may be used after an introduction, after the salutation in a business letter, before an example, explanation, or statement, and separates hours from minutes.

4. **Dash (—)**: used to show interjected thoughts, sudden change in statement, and sometimes something similar to an example within a sentence.

5. **Ellipsis (...)**: indicates omission of one or more words in a quoted sentence or several words or sentences within any quotation.

6. **Exclamation Point (!)**: ends a word, phrase, or sentence while indicating surprise or some type of strong emotion.

7. **Hyphen (-)**: connects a word which has part of its letters, ending with a complete syllable, on one line and the rest of the word on the

next line. It is also used to connect the elements of a compound word.

8. **Parentheses ( )**: enclose a word or phrase within a sentence or a sentence or sentences within a paragraph that is/are not necessary to complete either the sentence or paragraph. Most often, the parentheses enclose supplementary information. Brackets [ ] normally indicate supplementary information included by the editor rather than by the author.

9. **Period (.)**: marks the end of the majority of sentences, is used for abbreviations, and separates whole numbers from decimal fractions.

10. **Semicolon (;)**: joins independent clauses in a compound sentence and joins a succession of phrases in a sentence. It is used as a substitute for a coordinating conjunction. As a reading signal or a writing tool, the semicolon has more "pause power" than the comma and allows for more connection or continuity than the period.

11. **Question Mark (?)**: ends a sentence requiring an answer. Some sentences may be stated in the form of a question but actually are statements. Unless the sentence requires an answer, do not use a question mark.

12. **Quotation Marks (" ")**: used to enclose a character's dialogue, direct quotations, aphorisms, and unconventional words and phrases. Whenever there is a quotation within a quotation, the primary quotation is enclosed by double marks (" "), and the quotation included within the primary quotation is enclosed in single quotation marks (' ').

13. **Indention or Double-spacing between Lines** : (Indention or five spaces):

____

____

____

(Double-spacing between Lines):

____

____

____

____

Either indention or double-spacing between lines signals the beginning of a new paragraph. The physical signal to indicate a paragraph is an indention or double space between lines. The paragraph is used to signal a change in topic, a change of speakers in a dialogue, or simply to provide a "reader rest" in a long discussion of a single topic.

Indention and double-spacing between lines are also used to set off a longer quotation from the body of a paper. Again, indention or double-spacing signals a type of change, in that case, the change from the writer's words to someone else's words.

SENTENCE ELEMENTS

1. **Subject**: what the sentence is about. Usually, the subject of a sentence is a noun, pronoun, pronoun phrase, or noun phrase.

2. **Predicate**: the part of the sentence that contains the verb. A predicate contains a verb and may contain all the other types of words. The predicate usually says something about the subject of the sentence.

3. **Phrase**: a group of grammatically related words that does not contain a subject and a predicate.

4. **Clause**: a group of related words that contains a subject and a predicate.

5. **Independent Clause**: a group of related words that contains a subject and a predicate and expresses a complete idea.

6. **Subordinate Clause**: a group of related words that contains a subject and a predicate but does not express a complete idea by itself.

7. **Appositive**: a noun or noun phrase following a noun, noun phrase, or pronoun that in some way renames the noun in front of it. Syntactically, the construction looks like this: noun, appositive. An appositive always refers to the noun, noun phrase, or pronoun in front of it.

8. **Parenthetic Words, Phrases, and Clauses**: a word, phrase, or clause that is added to the fundamental sentence but is not necessary to complete the meaning of the sentence. A parenthetic word, phrase, or clause adds additional information that is unnecessary to the essential meaning of the sentence. However, parenthetic expressions in sentences can be very useful when an author wishes to include additional information.

SENTENCE STRUCTURES

1. **Sentence**: a group of grammatically related words that expresses one or more complete ideas.

2. **Simple Sentence**: a group of related words that expresses a complete idea. A simple sentence should have one independent clause. It may have additional phrases, but it cannot contain more than one clause.

3. **Compound Sentence**: two or more independent clauses or two or more simple sentences joined together by a coordinating conjunction and punctuated as one sentence. A compound sentence must contain two independent clauses and usually one coordinating conjunction. It may have additional phrases, but it normally does not have more than two independent clauses. (See "Run-on Sentence.")

4. **Complex Sentence**: one independent clause and one or more subordinate clauses that are punctuated as a single sentence. A complex sentence may contain a subordinating conjunction and additional phrases, but it cannot have more than one independent clause.

5. **Compound-complex Sentence**: two or more independent clauses and one or more subordinate clauses that are punctuated as a single sentence. A compound-complex sentence normally should not contain more than two independent clauses because the length of the sentence might lead to reader confusion.

POOR SENTENCE STRUCTURES

1. **Incomplete Sentence**: a word or group of grammatically related words that does not express a complete idea. An incomplete sentence may be a word, phrase, or a subordinate clause. Occasionally, an independent clause can be found in an incomplete sentence. However, such sentences contain additional words, phrases, or clauses which prevent the entire sentence from expressing a complete idea.

2. **Run-on Sentence**: a sentence that is actually two sentences run together. If two simple sentences are placed together without a coordinating conjunction or a semicolon, it is called a run-on sentence. If two or more independent clauses are placed together without a coordinating conjunction or a semicolon, it is called a

run-on sentence. The only time run-on sentences may be used occurs when three or more parallel clauses are closely related in meaning and structure.

TYPES OF SENTENCES

1. **Declarative sentence**: a sentence that states a fact, condition, idea, or possibility. Declarative sentences are the most common type of sentence. They end with a period (.) .

2. **Interrogative sentence**: a sentence that asks a question that needs an answer. Interrogative sentences end with a question mark (?) .

3. **Exclamatory sentence**: a sentence that expresses any strong feeling, from anger to surprise. Very often, an exclamatory sentence indicates surprise. Exclamatory sentences end with an exclamation mark (!) .

4. **Imperative sentence**: a sentence that makes a command, strong request, or issues an order. Imperative sentences end with a period (.) .

PUNCTUATION DEFINED

Punctuation is the writer's means of giving the reader signals for better reading. In oral reading we can hear those signals. They include audible stops, pauses, rising voice, falling voice, clipped words, contractions—in short, the sound of surprise, anger, questioning, the happiness of a game won,and even dialect. As readers we must attend to the writer's signals because our books cannot speak with audible words. As writers we must give our readers the signals they need to comprehend what we are trying to say. Without punctuation our writing may not show the reader our intent. Without punctuation writing may be very difficult to read.

The following quotation should show you how difficult it is to read something without punctuation. First, try to read this just as it is written. Then, after going through this passage, reading it as quickly as you can, go back over it and try to put all of the capitals, periods, commas, and any other form of punctuation you think belongs in the sentences, at the end of sentences, and at the beginning of sentences.

If you see a need to further divide this quotation by using paragraphs, write a ¶ in front of the first word you think should begin a paragraph.

PLEASE DON'T ASK ANYONE TO HELP YOU WITH THIS QUOTATION. YOU NEED TO KNOW WHAT YOU ALREADY UNDERSTAND AND, JUST AS IMPORTANT, WHAT YOU DON'T KNOW. OTHERWISE, YOU MAY BE UNAWARE OF YOUR OWN STRENGTHS AND WEAKNESSES.

this is a book about art and artists the artists painted cities under the ocean sea nymphs who softly spoke to the lost sailors monster sea serpents that crushed ships to splinters and fresh waterfalls on shore that awaited the terrified swimming sailors but our artists painted much more than just pictures our artists are creative so creative that many people say those artists are living examples of imagination in action art experts call the work of our artists incredible fantastic wonderful and sensual all of the art critics agree that our artists bring us sensational fantasy indeed those artists works are fantastically sensual our artists involve all of our senses through their art we can hear the waves crashing we tremble when we see the power of the sea serpents crushing the sailors ships we struggle with the sailors grasping and swimming to reach the safety of the shore bright colors reflect the depth of the ocean the threat of the sea shining colors take our thoughts to the warm sunlit shore color and form merge and bring us mythical images of good and evil might and vulnerability long hidden primitive thoughts and fears are powerfully felt by each of us as we view this art because unconscious thoughts are born to consciousness magical tales of men and monsters who live within come alive in each minds eye

After trying to read the selection without any punctuation or capitalization, you probably realize that punctuation makes reading easier. Punctuation simply gives us the signals to make reading sensible. Anything written is intended to be read. It may be something that thousands of people will read. It may be something very private that only the writer will read. But if it was written, someone must read it, even if it is only the writer. Punctuation, therefore, should be used to make the reading easier and quicker.

Now see how much easier it is to read the same selection when it is punctuated:

This is a book about art and artists. The artists painted cities under the ocean; sea nymphs who softly spoke to lost sailors; monster sea serpents that crushed ships to splinters; and fresh waterfalls on shore that awaited the terrified, swimming sailors. But our artists painted much more than just pictures.

Our artists are creative, so creative that many people say those artists are living examples of imagination in action. Art experts call the work of our artists "incredible," "fantastic," "wonderful," and "sensual." All of the art critics agree that our artists bring us sensational fantasy.

Indeed, those artists' works are fantastically sensual. Our artists involve all of our senses through their art. We can hear the waves crashing. We tremble when we see the power of the sea serpents crushing the sailors' ships. We struggle with the sailors grasping and swimming to reach the safety of the shore. Bright colors reflect the depth of the sea, the threat of the sea. Shining colors take our thoughts to the warm, sunlit shore.

Color and form merge and bring us mythical images of good and evil, might and vulnerability. Long hidden primitive thoughts and fears are powerfully felt by each of us as we view this art. Because unconscious thoughts are born to consciousness, magical tales of men and monsters who live within come alive in each mind's eye.

THESE POSSIBILITIES WILL SHOW YOU JUST HOW FLEXIBLE PUNCTUATION IS AS A TOOL:

This is a book about art and artists. (*A series of phrases or clauses is easier to read if you separate your series with semicolons. Semicolons provide a more definite "reader pause" than commas.*) The artists painted cities under the ocean; (*Could be a comma, but semicolon is better.*) sea nymphs who softly spoke to lost sailors; (*Could be a comma, but semicolon is better.*) monster sea serpents that crushed ships to splinters; (*Could be a comma, but semicolon is better.*) and fresh waterfalls on shore that awaited the terrified, (*If you can use* and *between two words, you need a comma.*) swimming sailors. (*That period could be a comma or semicolon. The sentence would not then be a run-on sentence.*

However, the sentence would be far too long and awkward. You would make reading difficult for your reader.) But our artists painted much more than just pictures.

Our artists are creative, so creative that many people say those artists are living examples of imagination in action. Art experts call the work of our artists "incredible," "fantastic," "wonderful," and "sensual." (*This series only needs commas to separate the series of words. The brief reading pause that a comma indicates is all that we need.*) All the art critics agree that our artists bring us sensational fantasy. (*Many writers would combine these first two paragraphs—they could be one paragraph.*)

Indeed, those artists' works are fantastically sensual. Our artists involve all of our senses through their art.(*Adverbial connectives are followed by a comma if they are the first word of a sentence.*) We can hear the waves crashing. (*Could be a semicolon.*) We tremble when we see the power of the sea serpents crushing the sailors' ships. (*Could be a semicolon.*) We struggle with the sailors grasping and swimming to reach the safety of the shore. (*If we combined the last three sentences, we would emphasize the interrelationship of "crashing," "crushing," "grasping and swimming."*) Bright colors reflect the depth of the sea, the threat of the sea. Shining colors take our thoughts to the warm, sunlit shore. (*Again, if you can use* and *between two words, you need a comma. In our first paragraph, "terrified, swimming" modified "sailors." All "modified" means is "affects." For example, a white cake is different from a chocolate cake. White modifies cake. Chocolate modifies cake.*) (*Some writers would also combine this last paragraph with the other two paragraphs.*)

The following discussion and examples are intended to help you with your punctuation. Some of the examples can be understood the first time you read through them. Other parts of the discussion and examples may need to be read several times. If you do not understand how something works, read over it again. Do not give up the first time through this information, and ask questions about anything you do not understand.

THE SIMPLE SENTENCE

Begin each simple declarative sentence with a capital letter, and end it with a period. You may not need any other punctuation, but if you have a series in the subject or a series in the predicate, you will need commas.

The simple sentence is the basic sentence unit. But understanding it thoroughly will help you with other sentence patterns. A simple sentence must have a subject and a verb. A simple sentence forms a complete idea. A simple sentence may be the same as an independent clause. It can stand by itself because it states a complete idea. The simple sentence and independent clause make sense when they are read individually. No other words are necessary to complete the idea or statement.

In all of the following sample sentences, the sentence begins with a capital letter and ends with a period. The capital and period in each sentence tell the reader where to begin and end a unit that forms a complete idea. All of these simple sentences may be called independent clauses.

The Simple Sentence: 1 Pronoun; 1 Verb

In the following sentences, the subject is one word, a pronoun. The verb unit is one word, a verb. The subject is underlined. The verb is circled.

Examples:

I worked hard. He came home. She stays at home

They study in the library.

The Simple Sentence: 1 Pronoun; 1 Verb Phrase (1 Independent Clause)

Subjects often require *be* words to express a complete idea. When *be* verbs are used, they may need another verb to complete the thought. The present tense *be* verbs are *am, is, are.*The past tense *be* verbs are *was, were.* A verb phrase is formed when a verb is joined with an auxiliary verb. The verb phrase is circled.

Examples:

I am working hard. He is coming home.

subject *predicate* *subject* *predicate*

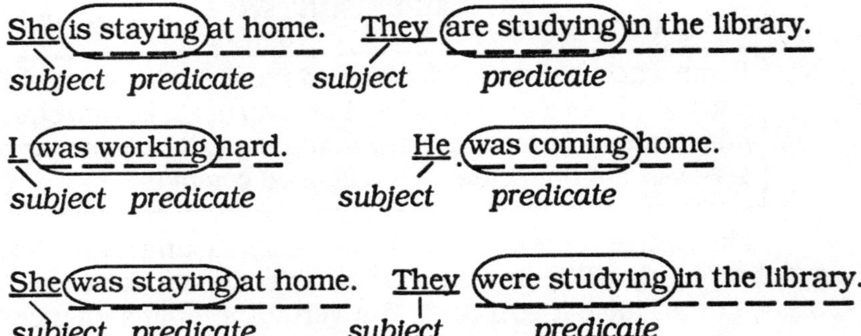

The Simple Sentence: 1 Noun or 1 Article and Noun; 1 Verb or Verb Phrase (1 Independent Clause)

In each of the following examples, the subject is a noun. You should also notice that the words *the*, *a* and *an* may function as part of the subject. The verb unit is formed by one, two, or three verbs. The verb phrase is circled.

Examples:

Joe went to school. The boy is reading.
subject predicate subject predicate

A girl will be swimming tonight. An apple was chosen.
subject predicate subject predicate

The second, third, and fourth sample sentences have verb phrases. A verb phrase has a main verb and one or more auxiliary verbs. Each of the sample sentences has only one subject and one verb unit. Therefore, all of the examples are still simple sentences.

The Simple Sentence: 2 or more Words as Subject; 1 Verb (1 Independent Clause)

Some simple sentences may have two or more words as subjects. Such sentences are simple sentences. The following sentences are simple sentences with more than one word as subject. The verb is circled.

Examples:

Bill and I are hungry.
subject predicate

Subject: 1 proper noun and 1 pronoun

Jim and Joe and John (jumped) on their horses.

subject *predicate*

Subject: 3 proper nouns

The bedroom, kitchen, and bathroom (are) clean.

subject *predicate*

Subject: 3 nouns with an article

The Simple Sentence: 1 Noun or Pronoun as Subject; 2 Separate Verbs

The following sentences are simple sentences with more than one verb in the predicate. That does not change the type of sentence structure. They remain simple sentences. They make a distinct statement. The verb is circled.

Examples:

We (ran) and (jumped) all the way home.

subject *predicate*

Verb Unit: "ran and jumped"

Joe (brushed) and (combed) his hair.

subject *predicate*

Verb Unit: "brushed and combed"

They (ate) and (drank) that night.

subject *predicate*

Verb Unit: "ate and drank"

The Simple Sentence: 2 or 3 Words as Subject; 2 or 3 Separate Verbs (1 Independent Clause)

Simple sentences can have more than one word in both the subject and the verb unit. Verb units are circled.

Examples:

Bill and I (ate) and (drank) that night.

subject *predicate*

Subject: proper noun and pronoun Verb: "ate and drank"

Jim and Joe brushed and combed the dog.

subject *predicate*

Subject: 2 proper nouns
Verb: "brushed and combed"

The bedroom, kitchen, and bathroom

subject

have been swept, scrubbed and waxed.

predicate

Subject: 3 common nouns
Verbs: "have been swept, scrubbed, and waxed"

In all of the examples of simple sentences, the sentence begins with a capital and ends with a period. Each sentence is a statement, and each sentence is a complete idea. No other words are needed to complete the statement or idea. Only the few sentences with a series of more than two words require commas.

More Complicated Simple Sentences

Simple sentences containing only a simple subject and a simple predicate without a series need to begin with a capital letter and end with a period. (1 Independent Clause)

Review Examples:

Her dress is lovely. Joe directed the caucus.

subject *predicate* *subject* *predicate*

Democracy may be total or limited.

subject *predicate*

Geometric designs are the best.

subject *predicate*

Simple sentences containing a series in the subject, predicate, or both need commas to separate the series. (1 Independent Clause)

Review Examples:

Mustard, lettuce, and tomatoes are great on hamburgers.

subject *predicate*

A quiche Lorraine is made with cheese, eggs, and a pastry shell.
subject *predicate*

Good Mexican tacos, enchiladas, and posole
subject
are made with lots of onions, meat, and chili.
predicate

Simple sentences may be expanded by adding phrases. The more complicated simple sentences that we will examine have been expanded to contain more information by adding phrases.

Simple sentences may also be expanded by adding words. The first sentences that we will be examining have introductory words. Punctuation of those is the easiest, but if you thoroughly understand how to punctuate sentences with introductory words, that will help you punctuate the more complicated sentences containing phrases. Just remember, all of the sentences that we will discuss in this section are simple sentences.

> *A sentence beginning with an introductory word usually needs a comma following the introductory word.*

Introductory words are used for three purposes:

1. An introductory word may modify the sentence which follows it.
2. An introductory word may serve to connect the ideas in the sentence before it and the sentence that follows it.
3. An introductory word may be nothing more than an interjection that may intensify or emphasize the meaning of the independent clause which follows it.

> *If an introductory word modifies the entire independent clause that follows it, the introductory word should have a comma after it.*

The comma signals a slight pause that emphasizes the effect of the introductory word on the independent clause. (Introductory Word, 1 Independent Clause)

Examples:

Laughing, they threw Mike into the river. (verbal introductory
subject *predicate* word)

Dying, she closed her eyes. (verbal introductory word)

subject *predicate*

Unfortunately, Bryan got a haircut.

subject *predicate* (adverbial introductory word)

If the introductory word is used to connect or relate the ideas in the sentence before it and the one that follows it, the introductory word should have a comma after it.

The introductory words most commonly used to connect or relate information contained in two separate sentences or independent clauses are called adverbial connectives or conjunctions. A brief review of adverbial connectives may remind you of the many times you have seen such words in your formal reading and writing. *Accordingly, consequently, furthermore, hence, however, indeed, in fact, nevertheless, therefore,* and *thus* are all adverbial connectives or conjunctions. To see how those words function in sentences, we will examine some sentences containing them. Please notice how those words can be used to relate information and ideas. We will discuss more about their use in your own writing under "Related Writing.")

Examples:

Accordingly, he followed the directions.

subject *predicate*

She directed him to follow the directions of the medicine. Accordingly, he followed the direction. (*Notice the pretentious language.)*

Besides, I didn't have the money to buy it.

subject *predicate*

The color of the jacket was just right, but it didn't fit quite right. Besides, I didn't have the money to buy it.

Consequently, the lawyer decided to sue.

subject *predicate*

No settlement could be reached. Consequently, the lawyer decided to sue.

Furthermore, the decision (is) ridiculous.

subject predicate

Your idea to install the sewer above ground is unsanitary. Furthermore, the decision is ridiculous.

Hence, Mr. Stockton (passed) to another world.

subject predicate

Much pain and suffering were felt. Hence, Mr. Stockton passed to another world.

However, it (is) lovely.

subject predicate

The china cost far too much. However, it is lovely.

Indeed, man's greatest concern (should be) with other men.

subject predicate

Men should love and care for one another. Indeed, man's greatest concern should be with other men.

In fact, some objects (appear) to move faster than the speed of light.

subject predicate

There is a theory that asserts that no mass can travel faster than the speed of light. In fact, some objects appear to move faster than the speed of light.

Nevertheless, color (may exist) without light.

subject predicate

A person cannot see a color without light. Nevertheless, color may exist without light.

Therefore, qualities (can exist) without light or being seen.

subject predicate

Light only allows the viewer to see physical qualities of an object. Therefore, qualities can exist without light or being seen.

Mild exclamations and interjections may precede an independent clause, and the sentence will continue to be a simple sentence.

If an exclamation or interjection precedes the independent clause, the mild exclamation or interjection should have a comma after it.

Since mild exclamations and interjections add emotional words that do not change the meaning of a sentence, the exclamation or interjection should be followed by a comma to separate it from the rest of the sentence.

Examples:

interjection or exclamation

Yes, he (got) the job.

subject *predicate*

exclamation

Wow, what a great looking chick.

subject

interjection or exclamation

No, he (hates) carrots.

subject *predicate*

interjection

Well, I (guess) so.

subject *predicate*

The sentences could have an exclamation mark after the first word if the writer wanted to express stronger feelings or attitudes.

Direct Address

When a speaker is talking to another person and interrupts his sentence to speak directly to the listener, it is called direct address. (Nouns and pronouns in direct address are sometimes said to be in the vocative case, and anything in the vocative case is separated from the rest of the sentence by one or two commas.) A direct address is always separated from the rest of the sentence by a comma because the direct address is nonrestrictive—unnecessary to the meaning of the basic sentence. A person's name, nickname, or a noun phrase used to identify the person being addressed is not necessary to establish any of the meaning of the sentence when used as a direct address.

The following examples will show you how a direct address functions within a sentence.

Examples:

direct address
Honey, the car (won't) (start).
subject *predicate*

direct address
Dear child, it (was) so thoughtful of you to bring me a bouquet of
subject *predicate*
dandelions.
predicate continued

direct address
Mrs. Smith, your son just (spilled) his chocolate soda.
subject *predicate*

direct address
Grace, life (is) so dull without you.
subject *predicate*

direct address
Frank, I (could)n't (say) it better myself.
subject *predicate*

If a direct address precedes the independent clause, place a comma after the direct address.

Introductory Phrases

Introductory verbal phrases and longer prepositional phrases function the same way that introductory words do. However, before we discuss punctuation of introductory phrases, a definition of phrases may help you understand what they are. A phrase is a group of words that has no subject and predicate. If you will recall the discussion concerning clauses, you will remember that a clause has both a subject and a predicate. The subject of a clause can be formed by one or more words, and the predicate can be formed by one or more verbs and usually some additional words to expand the information of the clause.

A phrase, on the other hand, has no subject and predicate. A phrase is simply a group of grammatically related words that function together as a single unit. For instance, look at the phrase "on the other hand":

prepositional phrase

A phrase, on the other hand, has no subject and predicate.

subject *predicate*

The phrase "on the other hand" has no subject or predicate, but the words are related. In fact, they are so related that they act together as a single unit.

> *An introductory verbal phrase should be followed by a comma when it precedes an independent clause. A long introductory prepositional phrase should be followed by a comma if the words in the independent clause following it are in normal word order.*

Introductory Phrases; 1 Independent Clause:

We will examine some sentences to see how phrases are composed of related words that have no subject and predicate. All of the sentences containing these phrases are simple sentences. Each sentence contains only one clause, and that clause is independent.

Examples:

(Usually, only a longer introductory prepositional phrase needs a comma following it. However, for emphasis a comma may be placed between a short introductory prepositional phrase and the independent clause.)

prepositional phrase

On the whole, your ship's design is very good.

(*comma optional*) *subject* *predicate*

(Any introductory verbal phrase should be followed by a comma.)

verbal phrase

Disgusted by the slaughter, she left the bull fight.

subject *predicate*

(A longer introductory prepositional phrase needs a comma following it.)

prepositional phrase

After an unusually cold and windy winter, spring came early.

subject *predicate*

Recognizing the difference between phrases and clauses is very important, for your knowledge of them will prevent you from writing incomplete sentences. Also, recognizing the difference between phrases and clauses will help you punctuate sentences correctly. A phrase cannot function as a sentence because it has no subject and predicate. It would not make sense to write a phrase as a sentence because a phrase does not make a complete statement. Read these phrases and see how easy it is to tell that a phrase can never function as a complete sentence.

Examples:

after the baseball game	(prepositional phrase)
starting a motor	(verbal phrase)
pleased with himself	(verbal phrase)

As you can see, each phrase leaves the reader wondering what is supposed to come next; the idea has not been completed. A phrase cannot function as a sentence simply because it does not express a complete idea. Any sentence must express a complete idea. Phrases are intended to add to the information contained in the sentences in which they are included; they are not meant to express a complete idea. Nevertheless, phrases are very useful, particularly for expanding the meaning of a sentence and connecting and varying a person's writing. Phrases are often used in the subject, predicate, or both.

Now we will return to our discussion of punctuation and introductory phrases.

An introductory verbal phrase should be followed by a comma when it precedes an independent clause.

Verbal phrases begin with some form of a verb, and the verbal phrase is followed by its modifiers. If you remember your verbs, verbal phrases will be easy to identify. The first word of a verbal phrase will end with *ing*, *ed*, or *en* forms or be an infinitive—an infinitive is the present tense of any verb preceded by *to*.

Examples of verbal phrases:

-ing	*-ed* or *-en*	*to* and *present tense verb*
running in the water	frightened by the water	to swim or sink
going over there	gone as a dream	to go over there
laughing through a huge red mouth	laughed at by all	to laugh through a huge red mouth
stopping quickly	stopped by the fast ball	to stop the fast ball
throwing the ball	thrown in the stadium	to throw the fast ball

Now we will look at how those verbal phrases work within sentences as introductory phrases. You should notice that all of these sentences are still simple sentences even though they have verbal phrases which increase their length. (Introductory Verbal Phrase, 1 Independent Clause)

Examples of simple sentences containing verbal phrases:

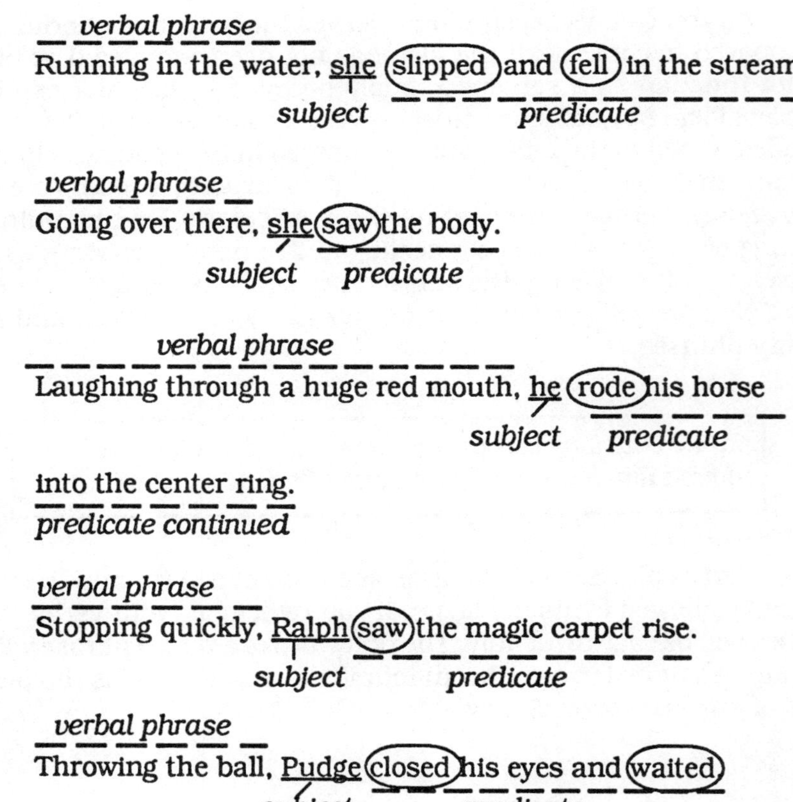

verbal phrase

Frightened by the water, she never (learned) to swim.

subject *predicate*

verbal phrase

Gone as a dream, the gentle young horse (sank) into the quicksand.

subject *predicate*

verbal phrase

Laughed at by all, the new clown (was) a great success.

subject *predicate*

verbal phrase

Stopped by the fast ball, Ralph (should have paid) attention

subject *predicate*

rather than watching the trick magic carpet rise.

predicate continued

> *A long introductory prepositional phrase, which may be a series of prepositional phrases, also needs a comma between it and the independent clause. If you wish to emphasize the importance of a short introductory phrase, you may also use a comma following the phrase. However, most introductory prepositional phrases that are short, usually one phrase long, do not need commas to follow them. Also, introductory phrases followed by the verb instead of the subject do not need commas to follow them.*

Longer introductory prepositional phrases are usually made up of a series of prepositional phrases. Since there is a series of prepositional phrases, the introductory part of the sentence is lengthened. The reason that a longer prepositional phrase is followed by a comma is to make the reading of the sentence easier. The comma simply provides a slight pause before the subject of a sentence, and that allows the reader to identify the subject of the sentence. Although a person may not be able to verbally identify a subject of a sentence, every reader must recognize something about the relationship of words within sentences to be able to read them so they make sense. The comma after a longer introductory phrase allows a reader to sense the subject of the sentence.

Before discussing punctuation of introductory prepositional phrases, they should be defined. Every prepositional phrase begins with a preposition, followed by a noun or pronoun; there may also be words that modify the noun or pronoun within the prepositional phrase. Words that show the relationship between the nouns or pronouns which follow them and other words within the sentence are prepositions. Some of the most common prepositions are these:

about	against	around	behind	between
above	along	at	below	beyond
across	amid	because of	beneath	but (except)
after	among	before	beside	by
concerning	inside	out	till	up
down	into	outside of	to	upon
during	like	over	toward	with
except	near	past	towards	within
for	of	since	under	without
from	off	through	underneath	
in	on	throughout	until	

Any of those words may serve as the first word in a prepositional phrase.

To better understand their punctuation, we will now examine some longer introductory prepositional phrases that need commas to follow them. Then we will look at some examples of short introductory phrases followed by inverted verbs and subjects. Again, those two types of introductory prepositional phrases do not need commas after them.

Examples of longer prepositional phrases that need commas to follow them:

series of prepositional phrases

In the barn near the stall beneath the water tank, you will find an extra large saddle.

preposition (In) — *preposition* (near) — *preposition* (beneath) — *subject* (you) — *predicate* (will find) — *predicate continued* (an extra large saddle.)

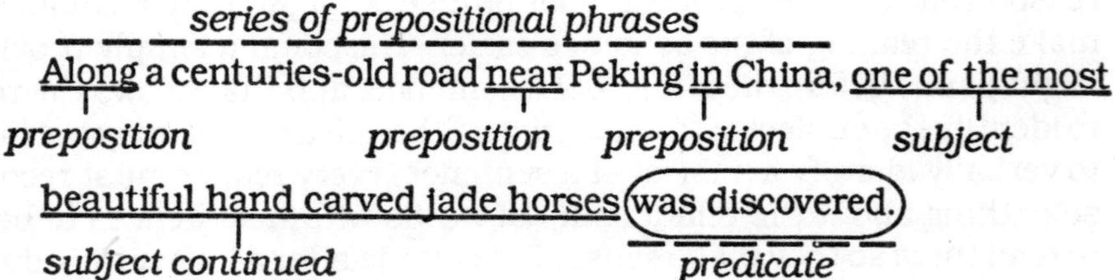

series of prepositional phrases

During prehistoric times within the United States up until the

preposition *preposition* *preposition*

modern geological age, small horses (roamed) our land.

subject *predicate*

series of prepositional phrases

Beneath the ocean near the coast of California, a wide variety of

preposition *preposition* *preposition* *subject*

shell fish (may be found.)

subject continued *predicate*

series of prepositional phrases

Among the flowers in the forest past Los Alamos, a strange white

preposition *preposition* *preposition* *subject*

one (looks) like crystal when washed by the morning dew.

subject continued *predicate*

series of prepositional phrases

Beyond Route 10 near Highway 70 outside of Borger, the race

preposition *preposition* *preposition* *subject*

(will be held.)

predicate

series of prepositional phrases

Within minutes after the departure on May 7th,

preposition *preposition* *preposition*

the conductor (made) an announcement.

subject *predicate*

noun clause (Notice that no comma is needed.)

In car twelve whoever was wearing the overpowering perfume

preposition *subject*

(would have to take) a shower or (get) off the train.

predicate

series of prepositional phrases

Inside the railcar near the last seat to the right,

preposition *preposition* *preposition*

a middle-aged man stood up and explained.

subject *predicate*

series of prepositional phrases

Before breakfast, during breakfast, and after breakfast,

preposition *preposition* *preposition*

I took showers.

subject *predicate*

series of prepositional phrases

Above my head, about my chest, across my chest,

preposition *preposition* *preposition*

my little grandaughter shot me with perfume.

subject *predicate*

series of prepositional phrases

From the seat in front of the smelly man, another man

preposition *preposition* *preposition* *subject*

pulled something from his briefcase and sprayed.

predicate

series of prepositional phrases

Among the passengers within the car near the man, the applause

preposition *preposition* *preposition* *subject*

rose.

predicate

parenthetic word

Big Help deodorant had saved the day and, thankfully,

subject *predicate*

our stomachs too!

predicate

As you may have been able to see, a comma following a longer prepositional phrase helps a reader correctly read such sentences. Again, the function of punctuation is to enable a reader to grasp quickly the correct meaning of a sentence. Commas must provide slight pauses which help a reader make sense out of a writer's writing.

Short Introductory Prepositional Phrases That May Need Commas

The great majority of the time, short introductory prepositional phrases do not lead to any type of reader confusion when the comma following the introductory phrase is omitted. In fact, the comma usually would just be unnecessary punctuation leading to slower reading. However, occasionally the arrangement of the words in a sentence may create a need for a comma to separate a short introductory prepositional phrase from the independent clause. (*A comma may also be used for emphasis.*)

> *If a short introductory prepositional phrase could confuse the reading of the sentence, use a comma to separate the introductory prepositional phrase from the subject.*

All of the following sentences need commas to clarify the meanings of the sentences. If you will read the following examples, you should be able to see why the commas help a reader read these sentences.

Examples:

In the air battles continue until death.
(*unclear*)

prepositional phrase
In the air, battles (continue) until death.
subject *predicate*

(Meaning: *someone or everyone dies when battles occur in the air.*)

prepositional phrase
In the air battles, (continue) until death.
predicate

The understood subject "you" could be placed before *continue*. (Meaning: *a command to fight to death. The sentence sounds like an order to a kamikaze pilot who was to make a suicidal crash on a target during W.W. II.*)

Some sentences are simply easier to read when there is a comma between the introductory phrase and the subject. Particularly when a noun ends the introductory prepositional phrase and a related noun begins the subject, a comma between the phrase and the subject may make the sentence easier to read.

> *If a noun ends the prepositional phrase and a related noun begins the subject, a comma between the phrase and the subject may make the sentence easier to read.*

Commas between the introductory phrase and the subject help clarify the meanings of the following sentences:

Examples:

During the revolution battles were fought with crude military equipment.

prepositional phrase
During the revolution, battles (were fought) with crude military
subject *predicate*
equipment.
predicate

In Santa Fe Pioneer Ware is doing well.

prepositional phrase
In Santa Fe, Pioneer Ware (is doing) well.
subject *predicate*

If you, as the author, have to read over one of your own sentences more than once which has an introductory prepositional phrase ending in a noun that is followed by the subject which is a noun, you probably need a comma. More than likely, if the sentence confuses you even momentarily, it will confuse your reader.

Other Short Introductory Phrases That May Need Commas Following Them

Reader confusion may result from other types of introductory phrases when there is no comma between the phrase and the subject. Therefore, a comma is useful after other short introductory phrases.

> *If a comma following an introductory phrase is necessary to help the reader determine the subject, place a comma between the introductory phrase and the subject.*

Commas help clarify the meanings of the following sentences as they are being read. If you will read the following examples, you should be able to see how the comma in each sentence helps the reader determine the subject of the sentence.

Examples:

When choosing people select friends with similar interests.
(unclear)

How do you recommend that I select guests for a party?

When choosing people, (select) friends with similar interests.
(understood subject "you") *predicate*
(answers question)

How do people choose their friends?

When choosing, people (select) friends with similar interests.
subject *predicate*
(answers question)

When observing the men stay inside of the planetarium.
(*Unclear: are the men doing the observing staying in the planetarium, or are the men going to be observed by someone inside of the planetarium?*)

When observing, the men (stay) inside of the planetarium.
subject *predicate*
(*Meaning: the men stay inside of the planetarium when they are observing.*)

When observing the men, (stay) inside of the planetarium.
(understood subject "you") *predicate*
(*Meaning: a command or suggestion to someone to stay inside of the planetarium when he is observing the men.*)

After baking cupcakes cool before frosting.
(unclear)

After baking cupcakes, (cool) before frosting.
predicate

(*understood subject "you"*)
(*Meaning: directions to someone to cool the baked cupcakes before they are frosted.*)

After baking, cupcakes cool before frosting.
subject *predicate*

(*Meaning: either the cupcakes cool before the frosting does or cupcakes cool before they are frosted. Unclear.*)

While growing onions protect roses from aphids.
(unclear)

While growing onions, protect roses from aphids.
(Understood subject "you") *predicate*

(*Meaning: suggestion that onions may bring aphids which should destroy the roses, so the grower should protect the roses.*)

While growing, onions protect roses from aphids.
subject *predicate*

(*Meaning: statement suggests that growing onions protect roses from aphids, which is true.*)

While racing cars use a special fuel.
(unclear)

While racing, cars use a special fuel.
subject *predicate*

(*Meaning: cars use a special fuel while they are racing, which is often true.*)

While racing cars, use a special fuel.
(understood subject "you") *predicate*

(*Meaning: a command or suggestion to use a special fuel while racing cars.*)

> *Any introductory element that contains a verb should be followed by a comma.*

Phrases that Function as Subjects: No Commas Needed

Whenever a verbal phrase is directly followed by the first verb of the predicate, the verbal phrase functions as the subject of the sentence. Therefore, a comma should not be placed after the phrase. To place a comma after the phrase would cut the sentence in half; it would actually divide the subject and predicate of the sentence. Do not place a comma after a phrase that functions as the subject of the sentence when the predicate immediately follows the subject.

If a verbal phrase is directly followed by the first verb in the predicate, do not place a comma between the phrase and the verb belonging to the predicate.

Some examples should help you see the syntactic features of a sentence in which a verbal phrase functions as the subject.

Examples:

To place a comma after the phrase would cut the sentence in half.
(phrase functions as subject) *predicate*

To place a comma after the phrase, would cut the sentence in half.
verb phrase
(As you can see, there is no subject following the verbal phrase, so the sentence is confused by the comma.)

phrase
Teasing my brother (is) fun.
subject *predicate*
(phrase functions as subject)

Teasing my brother, is fun.
(confused)

phrase
Washing behind my ears (is) a drag.
subject *predicate*
(phrase functions as subject)

Washing behind my ears, is a drag.
(confused)

Prepositional Phrases and Inverted Word Order: No Commas Needed

If a prepositional phrase is directly followed by the first verb of the predicate, the sentence is in inverted word order. That means the subject follows the verb. It also means that part of the predicate is in front of the subject.

Examples:

In the barn near the stall beneath the water tank (is) an extra large saddle.
preposition *preposition* *preposition* *subject*
predicate

Among the branches in the forest (sits) a robin.
preposition preposition subject
predicate

As you can see, a comma would just confuse such sentences.

Internal Punctuation of Simple Sentences

Simple sentences may also be expanded by appositives and other parenthetic words or phrases. Almost all appositives and all parenthetic words and phrases are nonrestrictive modifiers. Nonrestrictive modifiers add information to a sentence, but the information they add to a sentence is not necessary to complete the meaning of the sentence. If you will think of nonrestrictive modifiers as unrequired words that expand the information within the sentence, you should not have too much trouble identifying them. Since the information that a nonrestrictive modifier adds is unnecessary to complete the meaning of the sentence, the nonrestrictive modifier is enclosed within the sentences by commas.

It must be added that although nonrestrictive modifiers are not necessary to complete the main ideas of the sentence, they are very useful tools for adding information to all types of sentences. If they are not used so often that they become repetitive, they can help any writer say more in less space. In other words, nonrestrictive modifiers can be used to make a person's writing more concise and interesting.

> *Place a comma before and after a nonrestrictive modifier when the nonrestrictive modifier is in the middle section of a sentence.*

First, we will present a variety of nonrestrictive modifiers as they could be used within sentences. Then appositives and parenthetic statements within sentences will be examined separately. The last part of this discussion will bring appositives and parenthetic statements back together for a comparison of their similarities and differences.

Nonrestrictive Modifiers: Appositives and Parenthetic Statements

All of the nonrestrictive modifiers that will be used in the examples will be phrases because simple sentences are still being examined.

Examples:

appositive
Ice cream, my favorite treat, (is) delicious.
subject predicate

parenthetic statement

Frank, of course, becomes a recluse during the summer.

subject *predicate*

appositive

Mr. Eric Vanzura, our headmaster, plays tennis and stays

subject *predicate*

physically fit.

predicate, continued

appositive

Joe Cotruzzola, an English teacher, is touring Europe this summer.

subject *predicate*

parenthetic statement

A person's education, from birth to death, should remain a

subject *predicate*

pleasurable activity.

predicate, continued

appositive

The Dean of Students, Mr Suchland, seems mean but is an old softy.

subject *predicate*

appositive

Mark, the football star, should get more sleep.

subject *predicate*

appositive

The sisters, Mary, Wendy, and May, are making a quilt for the state fair.

subject *predicate*

appositive

The coelacanth, "the living fossil fish," has continued to exist for

subject *predicate*

millions of years.

predicate continued

appositive

"The Summer Birds," a story by Penelope Farmer, is an excellent

subject *predicate*

example of believable fantasy.

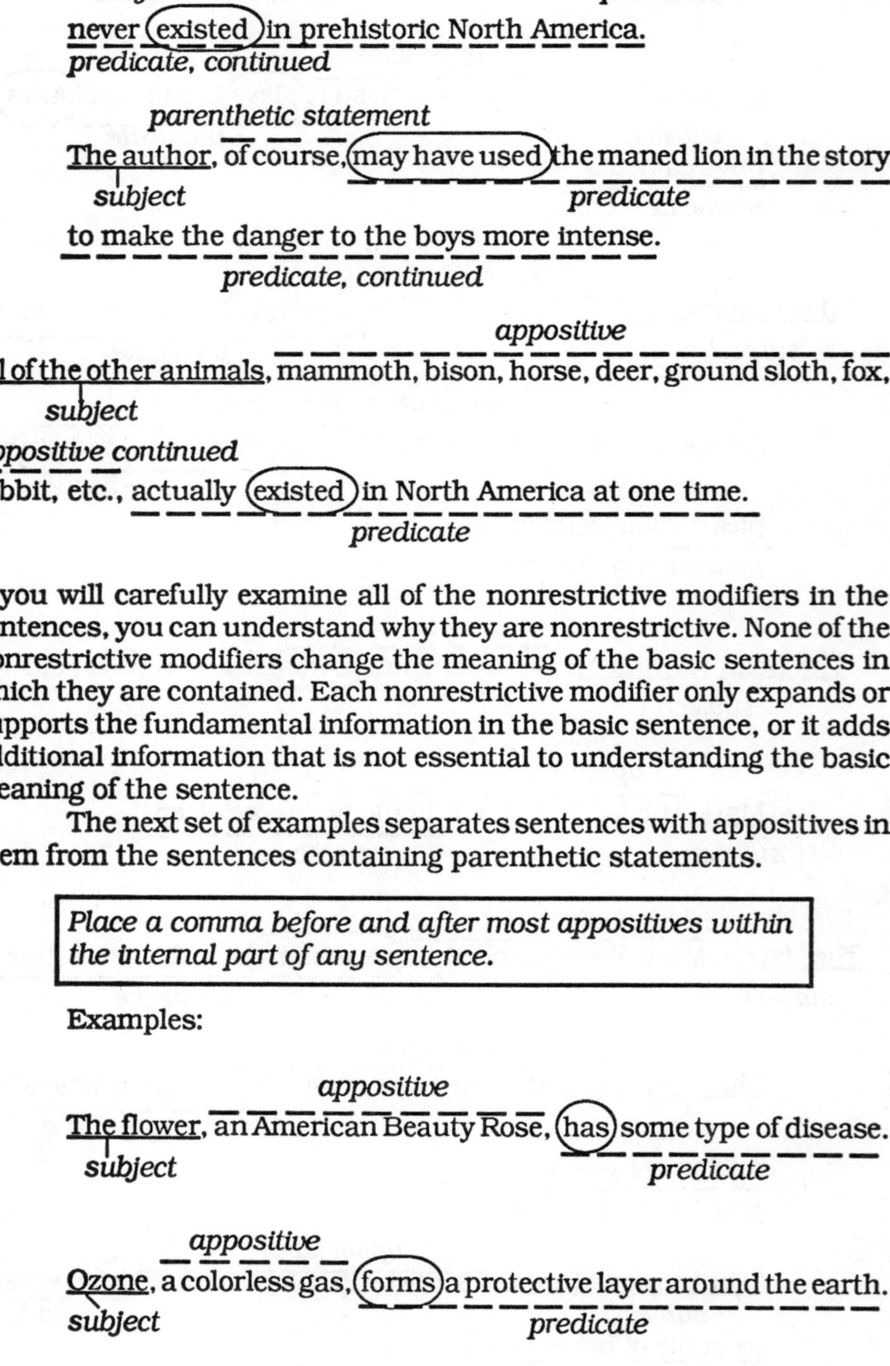

appositive

One animal, the maned lion, in "Beyond the Gorge of Shadows"

subject *predicate*

never (existed) in prehistoric North America.

predicate, continued

parenthetic statement

The author, of course, (may have used) the maned lion in the story

subject *predicate*

to make the danger to the boys more intense.

predicate, continued

appositive

All of the other animals, mammoth, bison, horse, deer, ground sloth, fox,

subject

appositive continued

rabbit, etc., actually (existed) in North America at one time.

predicate

If you will carefully examine all of the nonrestrictive modifiers in the sentences, you can understand why they are nonrestrictive. None of the nonrestrictive modifiers change the meaning of the basic sentences in which they are contained. Each nonrestrictive modifier only expands or supports the fundamental information in the basic sentence, or it adds additional information that is not essential to understanding the basic meaning of the sentence.

The next set of examples separates sentences with appositives in them from the sentences containing parenthetic statements.

Place a comma before and after most appositives within the internal part of any sentence.

Examples:

appositive

The flower, an American Beauty Rose, (has) some type of disease.

subject *predicate*

appositive

Ozone, a colorless gas, (forms) a protective layer around the earth.

subject *predicate*

appositive

The Egyptians (used) papyrus, a reed plant, to make a paper-like sheet

subject predicate predicate continued

on which to write.

predicate, continued

appositive

World War I, the war to end all wars, (was) the beginning of mechanized

subject predicate

military competition.

predicate, continued

appositive

Homer, author of the Iliad, (described) ancient galleys.

subject predicate

appositive

Galleys, slender ships propelled by oars during military action, (were) the

subject predicate

principle warships for over 2,000 years.

predicate, continued

appositive

The U.S.S. Long Beach, a guided missile cruiser, (was) the first nuclear-

subject predicate

powered ship.

predicate, continued

appositive

Winds and tides, the main forces previously used to move ships, (were)

subject

unreliable.

predicate

Place a comma before and after any parenthetic statement within the internal part of a sentence.

parenthetic statement

King Alfred the Great, after studying naval matters, (established) the first

subject predicate

full-time naval force in England.

predicate, continued

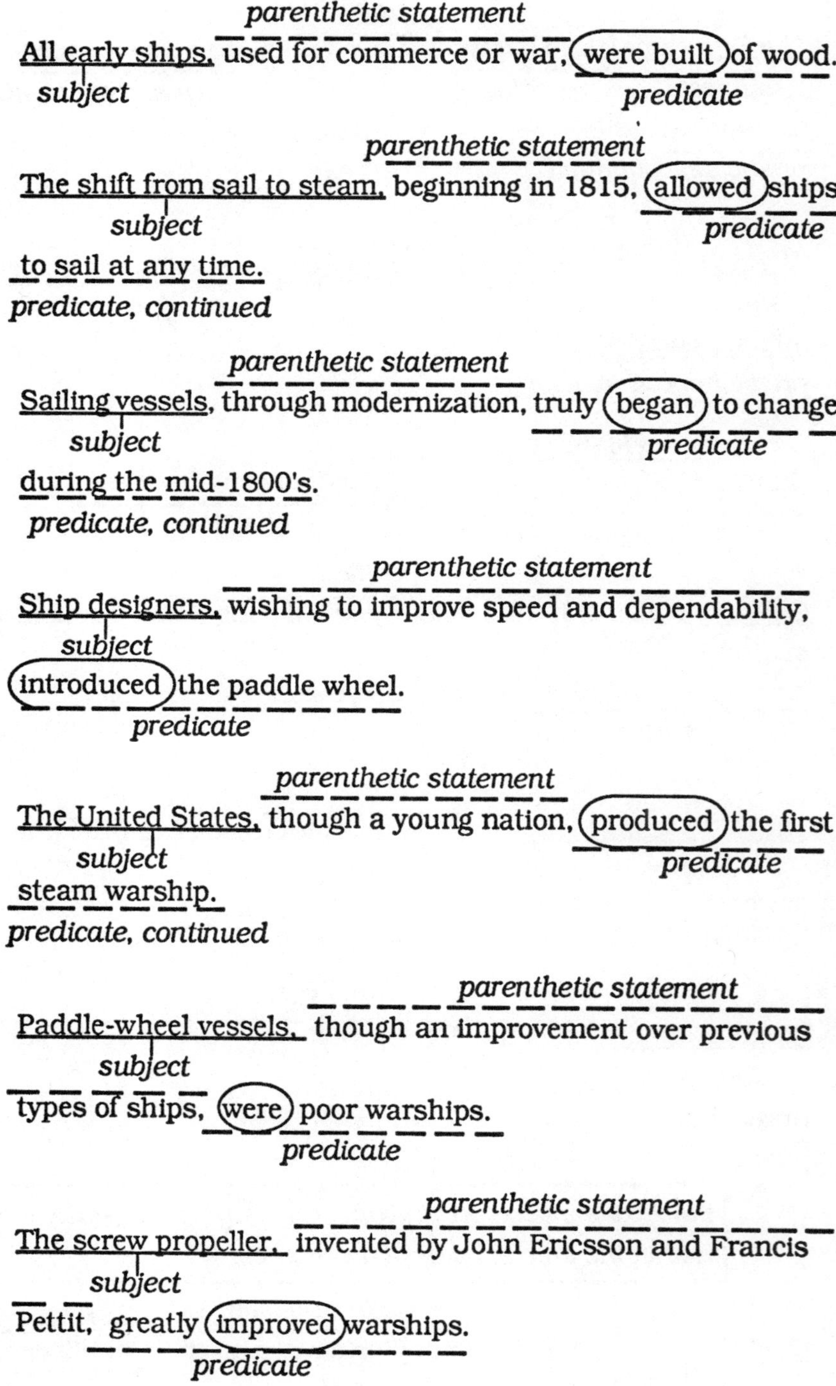
parenthetic statement
All early ships, used for commerce or war, were built of wood.
subject
predicate
parenthetic statement
The shift from sail to steam, beginning in 1815, allowed ships
subject
predicate
to sail at any time.
predicate, continued
parenthetic statement
Sailing vessels, through modernization, truly began to change
subject
predicate
during the mid-1800's.
predicate, continued
parenthetic statement
Ship designers, wishing to improve speed and dependability,
subject
introduced the paddle wheel.
predicate
parenthetic statement
The United States, though a young nation, produced the first
subject
predicate
steam warship.
predicate, continued
parenthetic statement
Paddle-wheel vessels, though an improvement over previous
subject
types of ships, were poor warships.
predicate
parenthetic statement
The screw propeller, invented by John Ericsson and Francis
subject
Pettit, greatly improved warships.
predicate

parenthetic statement

The iron hulls of armored vessels, popular from the mid-to-late

subject

1800's, produced the nickname "Ironclad."

predicate

Appositives

If you will go back to the examples containing the appositive for a moment and try a syntax game, you will find a sure way to distinguish an appositive from other sentence parts. Take the appositive and put it in the place of the noun or noun phrase that is just in front of the appositive .

Examples:

The flower, an American Beauty Rose, has some type of disease.

The flower, an American Beauty Rose, ...

An American Beauty Rose, the flower, ...

The Egyptians used papyrus, a reed plant, to make a paper-like sheet on which to write.

. . . papyrus, a reed plant, ...

a reed plant, papyrus, ...

If you have an appositive, you can always put it in the place of the noun or noun phrase and put the noun or noun phrase in the place of the appositive. In other words, the noun or noun phrase and the appositive are interchangeable.

Also, you can always eliminate either the noun phrase or the nonrestrictive appositive without changing the meaning of the sentence.

Examples:

The flower, an American Beauty Rose, has some type of disease.

The flower has some type of disease.

An American Beauty Rose has some type of disease.

Ozone, a colorless gas, forms a protective layer around the earth.

Ozone forms a protective layer around the earth.

A colorless gas forms a protective layer around the earth.

As you can see, an appositive says much the same thing as the noun or noun phrase in front of it; an appositive just adds additional information about the noun or noun phrase in front of it.

Parenthetic Statements

A parenthetic statement often may be placed in front of the word or word group following it.

Examples:

verbal phrase

Used for commerce or war, all early ships were built of wood.

subject predicate

verbal phrase

Beginning in 1815, the shift from sail to steam allowed ships to

subject predicate

sail at any time.

predicate, continued

However, before you think that parenthetic statements operate in the same syntactic way as appositives, you need to see what happens when we omit the parenthetic statement or the words that precede it.

Examples:

parenthetic statement

All early ships, used for commerce or war, were built of wood.

subject predicate

All early ships were built of wood.

subject predicate

parenthetic statement

Used for commerce or war, were built of wood.

subject missing predicate

parenthetic statement

The shift from sail to steam, beginning in 1815, allowed ships

subject predicate

to sail at any time.

predicate, continued

The shift from sail to steam allowed ships to sail at any time.

subject predicate

parenthetic statement

Beginning in 1815, allowed ships to sail at any time.

predicate

(subject missing)

From those examples you can see that a parenthetic statement does not function in the same way as an appositive. An appositive always refers to the noun or noun phrase in front of it. A parenthetic statement may add information about whatever is in front of it, modify the information in the entire sentence, or just add additional information. The syntactic functions of the appositive and a parenthetic statement are quite different.

Distinguishing Between Essential and Nonessential Information: Restrictive and Nonrestrictive

You can always find a nonrestrictive appositive or parenthetic statement within a sentence when you need to punctuate it correctly. All you have to look for is unnecessary information within the sentence. Information that is not essential to the basic meaning of the sentence should be enclosed in commas.

Restrictive Appositives

An appositive always gives additional information about the pronoun, noun, or pronoun phrase in front of it. That is the syntactic function of the appositive. However, while unnecessary information should be enclosed in commas, all appositives are not unnecessary.

Although you may never use an unnecessary appositive, you should be able to recognize one. Also, you should know that a necessary appositive is *never* enclosed in commas because it is essential to the meaning of the sentence.

Examples the following examples and you will see why such appositives are necessary.

Examples:

restrictive appositive

Ronald Reagan my brother has quite a different personality from

subject *predicate*

restrictive appositive

Ronald Reagan the President.

predicate, continued

Omit the appositives "my brother" and "the President" and try reading the sentence:

Ronald Reagan has quite a different personality from Ronald Reagan.

subject *predicate*

Obviously, the appositives are necessary to establish the meaning of the sentence.

restrictive appositive *restrictive appositive*

Brownie my dog likes Brownie the robin.

subject *predicate*

Omit the appositives "my dog" and "the robin" and the sentence reads:

Brownie (likes) Brownie.
subject *predicate*

The sentence in which the appositive has been omitted seems to indicate that Brownie likes himself.

Normally, such sentences would read:

My brother Ronald Reagan has quite a different personality from the President Ronald Reagan.

My dog Brownie likes the robin Brownie.

Disregarding which noun or noun phrase is used as the appositive, the writer should not use commas to enclose the appositive. The appositives are used for necessary identification because the names are obviously being emphasized. Which words are used as appositives would be up to the author. If the author wanted to emphasize the names, he would probably place the proper names first.

Restrictive Phrases

A parenthetic statement can do several things: (1) it can give additional information about the words in front of it; (2) it can simply give additional information that is related to the entire discussion in the sentence; or (3) it can be used to interject the author's opinion or words to get the reader's support. (One of the most common parenthetic expressions used to interject the author's opinion is "in my opinion." Phrases used to get the reader's support include "as you know" and "as you can see.")

A parenthetic phrase is always nonrestrictive. Because of its very definition, "parenthetic," it must be nonrestrictive. However, as you have seen with the appositives, some information may look as if it is nonrestrictive at first glance but turn out to be restrictive. Restrictive information should never be set off by commas because the commas would interrupt the meaning of the sentence.

Examine the sentences below, and you will see what happens when a restrictive phrase is enclosed by commas.

Examples:

The handbook costing $4.95 (is) probably the best text.
subject *predicate*

parenthetic

The handbook, costing $4.95, was a waste of money and time.
subject predicate

Which handbook would you consider the best?
(question)

The handbook costing $4.95 is probably the best text.
(answer)

The restrictive phrase "costing $4.95" is used to identify a particular text. Therefore, "costing $4.95" is necessary to the meaning of the sentence.

Which book was the poorest?

a. history text
b. physical fitness guide
c. English book
d. math handbook

The handbook, costing $4.95, was a waste of money and time.
(answer)

The phrase "costing $4.95" adds additional information that is not essential to the meaning of the sentence. Since the question only asked, "Which book was the poorest?" and nothing about the price, "costing $4.95" is nonrestrictive.

SUMMARY OF MECHANICAL RULES FOR DECLARATIVE OR IMPERATIVE SIMPLE SENTENCES

Capitalization

Begin each simple sentence with a capital letter.

Series

If the simple sentence contains a series of three or more words, separate the words with commas. Although the comma just before the conjunction in such a series is optional, it is usually best to place a comma before the conjunction.

Introductory Words

1. If an introductory word modifies the entire independent clause following it, the introductory word should have a comma after it.
2. If an introductory word is used to connect or relate the ideas in the sentence before it and the independent clause following it, the introductory word in the simple sentence should have a comma after it.

3. If a mild exclamatory or interjectional word precedes the independent clause, the exclamation or interjection should have a comma after it for mild emphasis.
4. If a direct address precedes the independent clause, place a comma after the direct address.

Introductory Phrases

1. If an introductory verbal phrase precedes the independent clause, the introductory verbal phrase should have a comma after it.
2. If the words in the independent clause following a long introductory prepositional phrase are in normal word order, a comma should be placed after the long introductory prepositional phrase.
3. If you wish to emphasize the importance of any short introductory phrase, you may use a comma following the phrase.
4. If a short introductory prepositional phrase would confuse the reading of the sentence, use a comma to separate the introductory prepositional phrase from the subject. If a noun ends the prepositional phrase and a related noun begins the subject, a comma between the phrase and the subject may make the sentence easier to read.
5. If a comma following an introductory phrase is necessary to help the reader determine the subject, place a comma between the introductory phrase and the subject.

Phrases That Function as Subjects; No Commas

If a phrase functions as the subject of a sentence, do not place a comma between the phrase and the verb belonging to the predicate.

Transposed Word Order; No Commas

If a simple sentence contains transposed word order, do not place a comma between the phrase and the main verb.

Internal Punctuation of Simple Sentences:

1. Place a comma before and after any internal appositive that simply adds additional information to the sentence.
2. Place a comma before and after any parenthetic statement within the internal part of a sentence.

QUESTIONS AND EXCLAMATIONS: INTERROGATIVE AND EXCLAMATORY SENTENCES

> *If a sentence asks a question that needs to be answered, it should end with a question mark. If a sentence is intended to show great emotion—surprise, disgust, or any very strong feeling - it should end with an exclamation mark.*

Our discussion and examples concerning simple sentences bring us to some other types of sentences. Basically, questions and exclamations are contained in all types of sentence structures. Sentences that ask questions are called interrogative sentences. Sentences that contain an interjection or a strong utterance are called exclamatory sentences. All that means is that a question should end with a question mark, and an exclamation should end with an exclamation point. Unlike the definition of the simple sentence which tells the writer the limits of the sentence, those definitions do not indicate much about the structure of such sentences. All we can tell is that any sentence must begin with a capital letter, so either type of sentence must begin with a capital letter. We can also tell what the end punctuation should be.

To determine what kind of internal punctuation an interrogative or exclamatory sentence needs, we must examine the sentence. First, we will look at interrogative and exclamatory sentences that have sentence parts similar to the simple sentence. The words may be in a different order or some words may be shortened, but the same ingredients are there.

As you read over these examples, please notice that each sentence has a subject and a verb or verb phrase. The subject and verb are still necessary to make the sentence make sense. Subjects are underlined, and verbs and verb phrases are circled.

Examples:

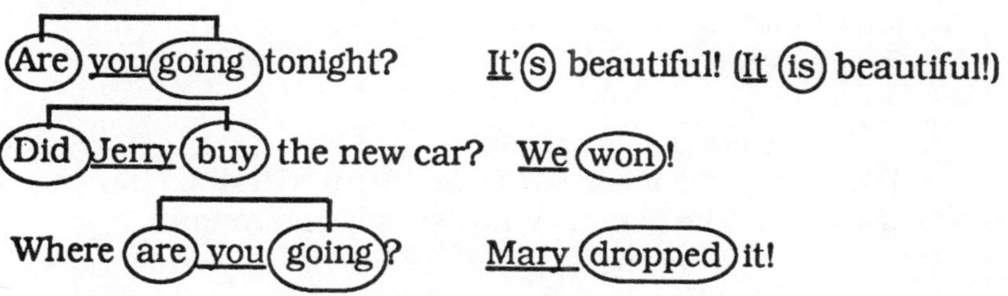

Those examples only show interrogative and exclamatory sentences in one type of sentence structure. As we said before, questions and exclamations can be contained in all types of sentence structures.

SENTENCES USED PRIMARILY IN DIALOGUE: UNDERSTOOD SUBJECT AND/OR VERB

Some sentences used in dialogue may be incomplete. They are just understood to be complete by the listener or reader. These are the only incomplete sentences which should be punctuated as if they were complete:

1. If a conversational but incomplete sentence makes a statement or issues a moderate command, capitalize it and end it with a period.
2. If a conversational but incomplete sentence asks a question, capitalize it and end it with a question mark.
3. If a conversational but incomplete sentence makes a strong command or is an exclamation, capitalize it and end it with an exclamation point.

Some sentences used in dialogue may be incomplete. They are completed by the reader's or listener's mind. The meanings of such sentences are implied by the speaker's or writer's conversation or situation before those sentences were spoken or written. They may not have a subject or verb, or they may even omit both the subject and verb. But they function like simple sentences. In such sentences, the subject, verb, or both subject and verb are understood to be there by the listener or reader. The writer or speaker does not include the subject, verb, or both because the reader or listener knows what should be there.

Sentences that have an understood subject and/or verb almost always occur in dialogue—the conversation part of a story or a discussion between people. Except when instructions are given, sentences with an understood subject and/or verb are not used very often in papers, articles, and textbooks. In stories of all types, they are appropriate.

Read the following sentences and see how they must be part of a conversation to make complete sense.

Examples:

Take out the trash.

(*You* or someone's name is the understood subject of that sentence. The sentence is a simple command.)

What?

(This could mean: "What did you say?" "What did you want me to do?" "What did she do?" It could also mean several other things. To understand that question, the reader or listener would have to know what has been said or done before that question was asked.)

Jerry!

(This could mean: "Jerry, you broke my favorite vase!" "Jerry, I'm so glad to see you!" It could mean several other things, too. Again, the reader or listener would have to know what had been said or what had happened before that exclamation could be thoroughly understood.)

Sentences with understood subjects, verbs, or both the subjects and verbs are necessary when you write stories or plays. They make the written words sound like speech, which is what they are supposed to do. Many times directions will omit the subject. Examine the sentence that was written before the examples: "Read the following sentences and see how they must be part of conversation to make complete sense." That sentence does not have a subject. The subject *you* is simply understood. Sentences with understood subjects, verbs, or both the subjects and verbs are appropriate in directions.

However, in essays, articles, and textbooks a writer usually does not use such sentences unless directions are being given. Too much is left out of such sentences. Omitting parts of sentences could interfere with the meaning the author wants to convey. In writing papers, articles, and textbooks, the author wants to be precise, so it is best to avoid such sentences in your papers. Also, by avoiding such sentences, you avoid writing incomplete sentences.

Incomplete sentences are sentences in which the subject, verb, or both have been left out. They may look exactly like sentences with understood subjects, verbs, or both the subjects and verbs. The big difference between an incomplete sentence and a sentence with an understood subject, verb, or both is the conversational character of the understood sentence. Understood sentences are supposed to sound informal. In more formal types of writing, the author's writing should appear more exact and precise. Incomplete sentences are not appropriate in papers. It is supposed to be the author who says exactly what he means. Unless the subject or verb is clearly understood, a group of words cannot stand as a sentence.

That does not change the usefulness of sentences with understood subjects, verbs, or both. Use sentences with understood subjects, verbs, or both subjects and verbs anytime you want your writing to sound like conversation. People talk using such sentences all the time. And such sentences are understood as being complete because the reader's or listener's mind puts in the missing parts. Just make sure that the missing parts are understood as being there. Otherwise, your writing will put too much of a burden on the reader.

Punctuate sentences with understood subjects, verbs, or both subjects and verbs as you would any other sentence:

1. A statement should end with a period (.).
2. A question should end with a question mark (?).
3. An exclamation should end with an exclamation mark (!).

THE COMPOUND SENTENCE

Once you understand the simple sentence, compound sentences are very easy to understand and punctuate. A compound sentence is nothing more than two simple sentences joined together by a coordinating conjunction.

As you have seen before, a simple sentence contains one independent clause. A simple sentence may also contain additional words and phrases. However, it cannot contain more than one independent clause. A sentence containing two independent clauses is called a compound sentence.

A compound sentence may be formed various ways:

1. A compound sentence may have nothing more than two independent clauses joined together by a coordinating conjunction:

(independent clause-coordinating conjunction-independent clause)

2. A compound sentence may have an introductory word or phrase, independent clause, coordinating conjunction, and another independent clause:

(introductory word-independent clause-coordinating conjunction-independent clause)

(introductory phrase-independent clause-coordinating conjunction-independent clause)

3. A compound sentence may have an appositive or parenthetic statement in either or both of the independent clauses that are joined together by a coordinating conjunction:

(independent, appositive, clause-coordinating conjunction-independent clause)

(independent, parenthetic statement, clause coordinating conjunction-independent clause.)

(independent, parenthetic statement, clause-coordinating conjunction-independent, appositive, clause.)

As long as there are two independent clauses joined together by a coordinating conjunction and no subordinate clause, the sentence is a compound sentence. You may add words or phrases to either or both of the independent clauses, and the sentence will continue to be a compound sentence.

If two short independent clauses are joined together with a coordinating conjunction, the comma may be omitted.

If two longer independent clauses are joined together with a coordinating conjunction, a comma should be placed before the conjunction.

And, but, or, nor, for, *and* yet *are coordinating conjunctions.*

Now some examples of compound sentences should be examined. If you have any real difficulty understanding the syntactic features of these compound sentences, you should review the section covering simple sentences.

The first set of examples will show some compound sentences in which the commas are optional; either the comma may be placed before the coordinating conjunction or left out.

Examples:

I did it and I'm glad.
subject *predicate* *subject* *predicate*

She came here and she cried.
subject *predicate* *subject* *predicate*

I thought so but I was wrong.
subject *predicate* *subject* *predicate*

Jerry spent the night and he slept well.
subject *predicate* *subject* *predicate*

The house was old and it was falling down.
subject *predicate* *subject* *predicate*

(Those sentences contain two independent clauses joined together by a coordinating conjunction. Remember, an independent clause always expresses a complete idea and can stand by itself without any additional words.)

The important thing to notice about the previous examples is that the meanings of the sentences were not confused because the commas were left out. The ideas, particularly the subjects, were so closely related that the omission of the comma did not confuse the sentence. A comma indicates a slight pause in a sentence, and those sentences did not need a pause to make them clear.

The next set of sentences will show two longer independent clauses joined together by a coordinating conjunction. These sentences need a comma before the coordinating conjunction.

Examples:

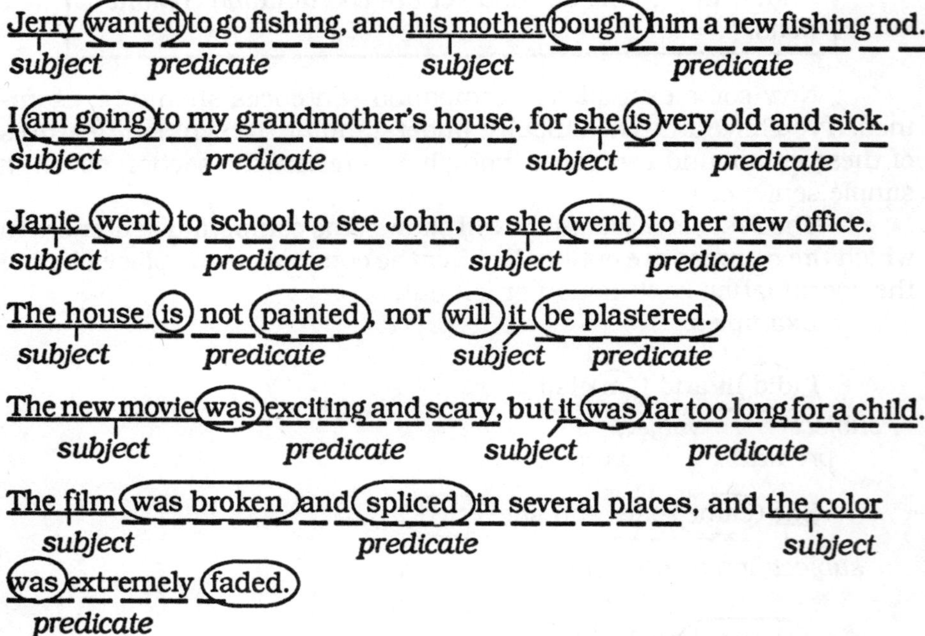

One thing that you may have noticed as you read the example sentences was that a slight pause was convenient. The pause created by the comma helps the reader sense the syntactic features of a compound sentence. Punctuation is intended to make written words readable just as the slight pauses in speech are there to help the listener.

Introductory Words and Phrases in Compound Sentences

Except for the comma placed before the coordinating conjunction between two longer independent clauses, which is a new form of punctuation to you, we have covered all the other forms of punctuation to be used in compound sentences. As you read through these examples, you will find that punctuation of compound sentences functions the same way as punctuation of simple sentences.

Examples of introductory words in compound sentences: (Place a comma after an introductory word used for emphasis.)

introductory word

Ugh, Vivian had on red lipstick, and she dyed her hair green.
subject *predicate* *subject* *predicate*

introductory word

Lovely, it (is) simply lovely, and it (is) so inexpensive.
subject *predicate* *subject* *predicate*

Examples of introductory phrases in compound sentences: (Place a comma after any introductory phrase that would require a comma in a simple sentence.)

verbal phrase

Gasping for breath, Judy (put) out the cigarette, and she
subject *predicate* *subject*

(promised) never to try another one of those horrible things.
predicate

introductory prepositional phrase

At the house next door to my sister's, the lawn (is) always green
subject *predicate*

and the roses (bloom) continually.
subject *predicate* *(No comma was placed before the coordinating conjunction because the independent clauses were short and their subjects closely related.)*

Examples of appositives in compound sentences: (Place a comma before and after any nonrestrictive appositive used internally in any sentence.)

appositive

Stew Little, the nutty guy in our class, (is) always (chasing) girls,
subject *predicate*

and he (won't ride) with any of the guys.
subject *predicate*

(Place a comma before and after any parenthetic phrase used internally in any sentence.)

parenthetic phrase

Santangel, believing in Columbus's idea, (raised) much of the
subject *predicate*

money needed for the voyage, but he (was) very disappointed by
predicate, continued *subject* *predicate*

the lack of the financial success of the voyage.
predicate, continued

Compound Sentences and Semicolons

Sometimes an author will join two independent clauses with a semicolon. The semicolon signals less of a break than a period, so it can signal a closer relationship between the information or ideas contained in two independent clauses. The semicolon also has more "pause power" than a comma, although it signals more connectedness than the period. Therefore, in a punctuation scale we might rate these punctuation signals as follows:

1. comma: slight pause; may be used to signal connection of ideas.
2. semicolon: moderate pause; may be used to signal connection of ideas.
3. period: long pause; usually signals the completion of a statement.

Keeping in mind the amount of pause each punctuation mark signals, we can summarize some general guidelines:

1. Use a comma and a coordinating conjunction between two independent clauses if you want the ideas or information in the separate clauses to flow together.
2. Use a semicolon between two independent clauses if you want to emphasize the connection between the information in the first and second clause while maintaining some separateness, perhaps for emphasis. However, do not use the semicolon too often, for the reader may ignore it as a signal for a moderate pause.
3. Use a period between two independent clauses if you want to signal a longer reading pause to emphasize separateness.

The semicolon is the punctuation mark to use when omitting the coordinating conjunction between two independent clauses in a single sentence.

Examples:

He wanted to win; he could lose.
subject predicate subject predicate

She wanted to lose weight; she gave up eating bread.
subject predicate subject predicate

The semicolon is the punctuation mark to use when joining an independent clause to another independent clause that is preceded by an adverbial connective.

Examples: (Please notice that the adverbial connective is not capitalized, and a comma follows it.)

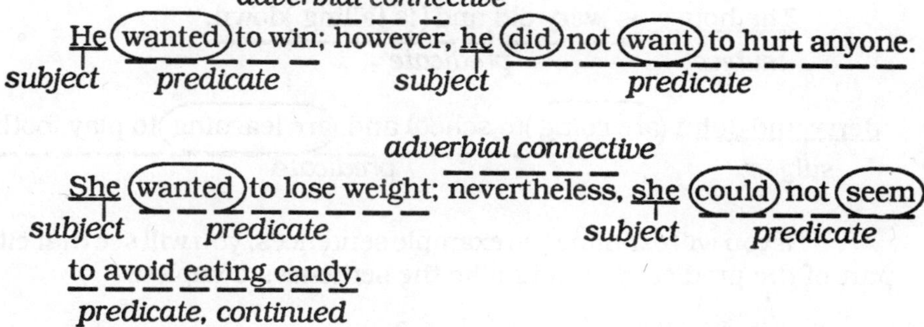

> *If the coordinating conjunction is omitted between two independent clauses containing closely related information, use a semicolon at the end of the first independent clause.*
>
> *If an independent clause is joined to another independent clause that is preceded by an adverbial connective, place a semicolon after the first independent clause and a comma after the adverbial connective.*

Anytime you want to determine whether a semicolon is used correctly, mentally place a period where your semicolon is placed. If the period is appropriate, so is the semicolon. Also, please remember not to capitalize the first word following a semicolon unless it is a proper noun.

Simple Sentences That May Look Like Compound Sentences

Some sentences may look like compound sentences at first. But if you examine them, you will find that they are not compound. Usually they are just simple sentences with compound predicates. They do not need commas or semicolons; do not confuse them with compound sentences. Examine the following sentences and see why they are not compound.

Examples: (How many subjects does the sentence have and how many separate predicates?)

Mary went to town and bought a new dress.
subject *predicate* *predicate*

(Are these separate predicates belonging to separate subjects, or are they compound predicates?)

He (went) fishing and (caught) his limit.
subject *predicate*

The house (is) very old and (is falling) down.
subject *predicate*

Jerry and John (are going) to school and (are learning) to play football.
subject *predicate*

If you will examine the example sentences, you will see that either part of the predicate would make the sentences complete:

Mary went to town.	Mary bought a new dress.
He went fishing.	He caught his limit.
The house is very old.	The house is falling down.
Jerry and John are going to school.	Jerry and John are learning to play football.

However, those sentences are not compound sentences. They would have to have two separate subjects attached to two separate predicates to be compound sentences. Each sentence simply has a compound predicate that could function as two separate predicates but actually functions as one predicate.

SUMMARY OF MECHANICAL RULES FOR DECLARATIVE OR IMPERATIVE COMPOUND SENTENCES

1. If two short independent clauses whose meanings are related are joined together with a coordinating conjunction, the comma may be omitted.
2. If two longer independent clauses are joined together with a coordinating conjunction, a comma should be placed before the conjunction.
3. Any nonrestrictive words or phrases should be separated from the independent clause in which they are contained by a comma or commas.
4. If the coordinating conjunction is omitted between two independent clauses containing closely related information, use a semicolon at the end of the first independent clause.
5. If an independent clause is joined to another independent clause that is preceded by an adverbial connective, place a semicolon after the first independent clause and a comma after the adverbial connective.

THE COMPLEX SENTENCE

A complex sentence contains one independent clause and a subordinate clause or clauses. Again, a subordinate clause contains a subject and a predicate but does not express a complete idea by itself.

The complex sentence has three basic types of construction:

1. A complex sentence can be formed with an independent clause and a subordinate noun clause.
2. A complex sentence can be formed with an independent clause and a subordinate adjective clause.
3. A complex sentence can be formed with an independent clause and a subordinate adverb clause.

As we will discuss later, a complex sentence may contain more than one subordinate clause and other nonrestrictive words and phrases. However, we will first examine the three basic types of construction that were listed above.

Examples of complex sentences containing noun clauses:

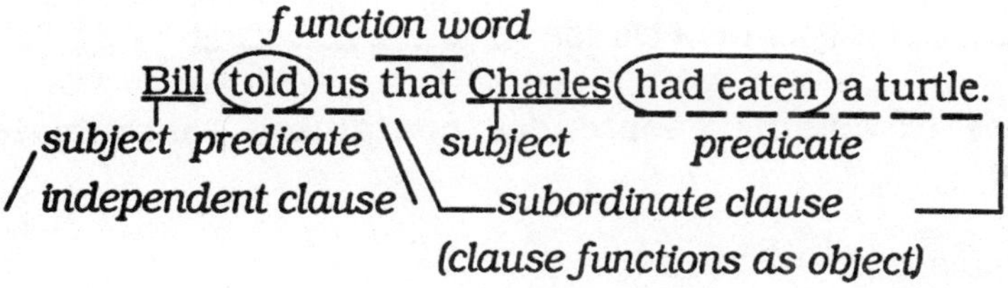

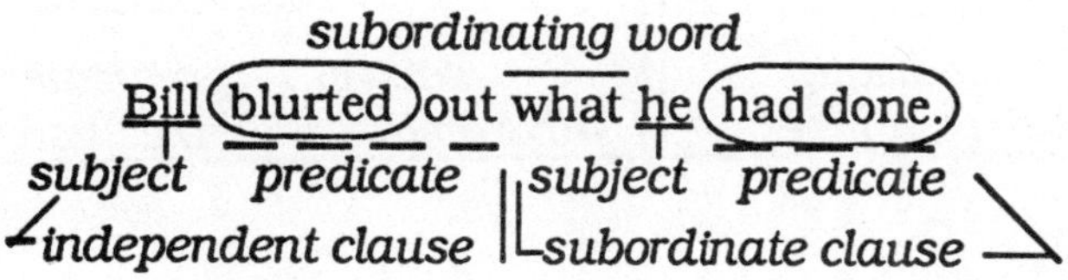

function word

Bill told us that Charles had eaten a turtle.

subject predicate *subject predicate*

independent clause *subordinate clause*

(clause functions as object)

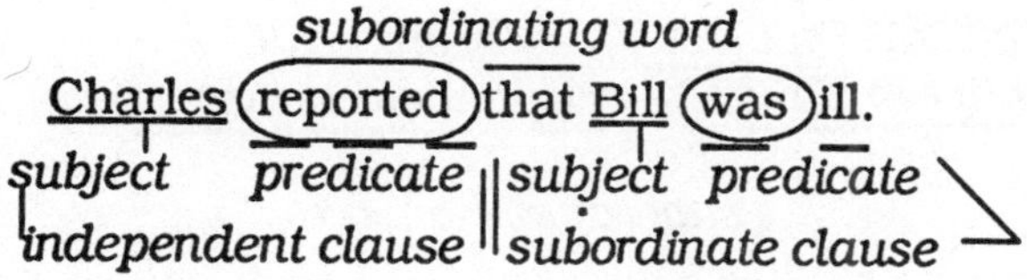

subordinating word

Charles reported that Bill was ill.

subject predicate *subject predicate*

independent clause *subordinate clause*

subordinating word

Bill blurted out what he had done.

subject predicate *subject predicate*

independent clause *subordinate clause*

Examples of complex sentences containing adjective clauses:

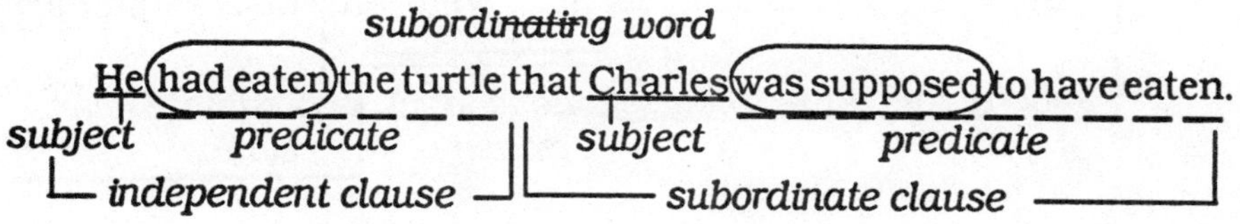

subordinating word

He had eaten the turtle that Charles was supposed to have eaten.

subject predicate *subject predicate*

independent clause *subordinate clause*

subordinating word *This entire clause functions to modify the subject.*

The turtle that was to be saved for the Queen's soup had been eaten.

subject *subject* *predicate* *predicate*

subordinate clause

independent clause

subordinating word

A turtle that is cooked may be good to eat.

subject *subject* *predicate* *predicate*

subordinate clause

independent clause

subordinating word

But a turtle that is alive may not be too digestible.

subject *subject* *predicate* *predicate*

subordinate clause

independent clause

Examples of complex sentences containing subordinate adverb clauses:

subordinating word

While I was fishing, I saw a sailboat turn over.

subject *predicate* *subject* *predicate*

subordinate adverb clause *independent clause*

subordinating word

The men began to yell for help because they could not swim.

subject *predicate* *subject* *predicate*

independent clause *subordinate adverb clause*

subordinating word

As they slowly began to sink, I saw why they could not swim.

subject *predicate* *subject* *predicate* *subject* *predicate*

subordinate adverb clause *independent clause* *subordinate noun clause*

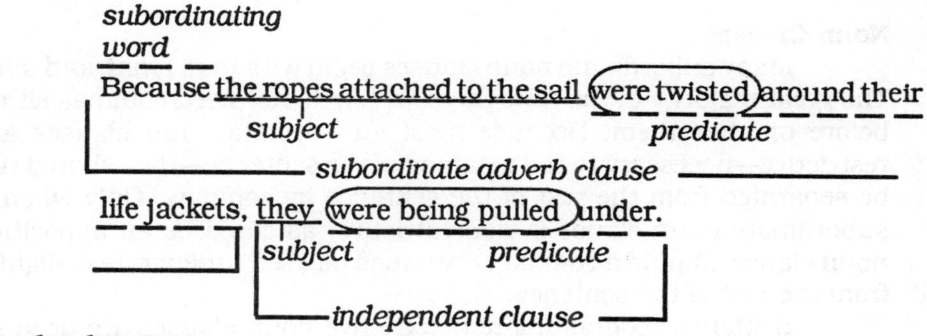

subordinating word

Because the ropes attached to the sail were twisted around their life jackets, they were being pulled under.

subject *predicate*

subordinate adverb clause

subject *predicate*

independent clause

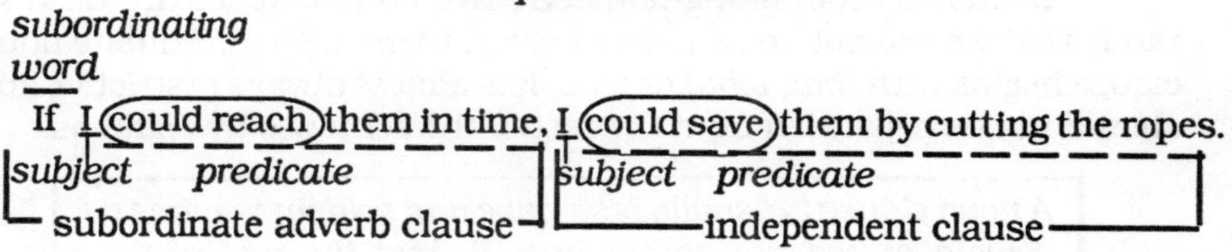

subordinating word

If I could reach them in time, I could save them by cutting the ropes.

subject *predicate* *subject* *predicate*

subordinate adverb clause — independent clause

In all of the preceding example sentences, one word made the subordinate clause dependent upon the independent clause. Anytime a word or phrase functions to make a clause dependent, the result is a subordinate clause. The most typical subordinating words are:

noun clause	adjective clause	adverb clause	
that	who	after	although
what	when	as	as if
when	whose	as soon as	because
where	which	as long as	lest
who	that	before	provided
whom	where	since	since
why		until	so that
whoever		when	though
whomever		whenever	unless
		where	whereas
		while	while
		if	whether or not

(*Often, the relative pronoun is omitted in sentences because it is " understood." See page 65 for an example sentence.*)

Noun Clauses

Many subordinate noun clauses begin with *that, what,* and *who.* The great majority of the time those words do not need commas either before or after them. Because most subordinate noun clauses are restrictive—necessary to the meaning of the sentence—they should not be separated from the rest of the sentence by commas. Only when a subordinate noun clause is nonrestrictive, as could be an appositive noun clause, should a comma or commas be used to separate it slightly from the rest of the sentence.

Sentences containing nonrestrictive noun clauses are used so rarely that we will not present examples of them. If a subordinate noun clause begins with *that, what* or *who,* it is almost always restrictive and should not be separated from the rest of the sentence by commas.

> *A noun clause is usually restrictive and seldom requires a comma or commas to separate it from the rest of the sentence.*

Adjective Clauses

A subordinate adjective clause should follow the noun it modifies so the reader can readily understand what the adjective clause modifies. The great majority of the time adjective clauses begin with *who, whom, whose, which,* or *that.* Those words are relative pronouns.

As you examine the example sentences, you should be able to see why an adjective clause begins with a relative pronoun and should follow the noun it modifies.

Examples:

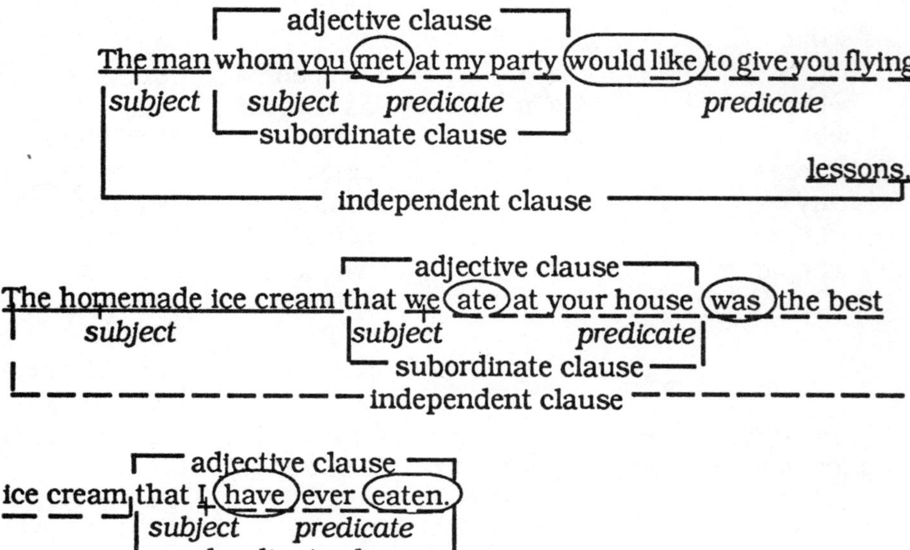

adjective clause
The fish that was caught turned out to be a coelacanth.
subject subject predicate predicate
subordinate clause
independent clause

As you can see, adjective clauses describe the nouns in front of them. Usually, adjective clauses are restrictive because they are used to identify more specifically the nouns in front of them. However, they can also be nonrestrictive. *Which* is often used to introduce nonrestrictive information.

Examine the question and answers that follow, and you should be able to see how to determine whether an adjective clause is restrictive or nonrestrictive.

Examples:

Has the bank moved?

nonrestrictive adjective clause
The bank, which used to be on 2nd and Central, has moved.
subject *predicate*

Where is my old bank?

restrictive adjective clause (*helps to identify "my old bank"*)
The bank that used to be on 2nd and Central has moved.
subject *predicate*

Was the gymnast any good?

nonrestrictive adjective clause
The gymnast, who was a girl, was exceptionally good.
subject *predicate*

Who was the best gymnast?

restrictive adjective clause (*helps identify "the best gymnast"*)
The gymnast who was a girl was exceptionally good.
subject *predicate*

Although you have seen that adjective clauses can be nonrestrictive because they may be useful as parenthetic statements, generally they are restrictive. If they were not needed to further identify the noun in front of them, most good writers would probably omit them. Therefore, most of the time when adjective clauses are used, they are restrictive. Being restrictive, an adjective clause would not need any commas to separate it from the rest of the sentence.

However, you must read a sentence to determine whether an adjective clause is restrictive or nonrestrictive.

> *If an adjective clause is restrictive (necessary), do not use a comma or commas to separate it from the rest of the sentence.*
> *If an adjective clause is nonrestrictive (unnecessary), use a comma or commas to separate it from the rest of the sentence.*

Adverb Clauses

As a writer matures, he learns to indicate all sorts of relationships through written words. An adjective clause is only one way of relating words to other words. An adjective clause is simply related to the noun in front of it; it is used to identify or further describe the noun.

Another type of clause, the adverb clause, is used to show time relationships or location, to establish cause and effect, or to indicate a contrast between statements.

As you may have noticed in the previous examples of complex sentences, one word usually functions to subordinate a clause. Since it is usually one word or phrase that makes one clause (the subordinate clause) dependent upon the independent clause, we will list some of the subordinating words for adverb clauses. We will also try to explain the functions of these words before the example sentences are presented.

Adverbs for Time Relationships and Location		Adverbs to Establish Cause and Effect or Indicate Contrast Between Statements	
Time Relationships:		although	whereas
after	since	as if	while
as	until	because if	whether or not
as long as	when	lest	if
as soon as	whenever	provided	if . . . then
before	while	since	
		so that	
Location:		though	
where		unless	
wherever			

Adverb clauses not only function to indicate relationships between ideas in sentences, but they also function to help relate sentences within paragraphs. In fact, many of the relationships between sentences within paragraphs are shown through adverb clauses and introductory words and phrases. As we go through the examples of adverb clauses, the sentences containing adverb clauses will be placed within paragraphs to show how they also relate sentences to other sentences. Each sentence below is a complex sentence containing an adverb clause. After you have read them in regular paragraph form, we will show you the

Examples:

Before our meeting officially began, our boss got up and made a speech to the employees. Because that speech changed most of the employees' views, I wanted to repeat it to you:

"After this plant was established, the owners decided to give 50% of the profits to the employees. No employee had to buy any stock in the company because motivation to do good work was considered as being the employee's part of the investment. As long as the employees realized that, the profits of the plant continually increased. Men and women spent extra time thinking about how to do a better job since they knew that they would receive their part of the profit. Furthermore, an employee rarely used all of his sick leave because he wanted to increase the profits of the plant and, therefore, his own profit.

"Although that profit sharing plan worked well during past years, it no longer seems to be working as well. Profit is down because employee production has declined. Unless profits increase, the company will have to discontinue the present profit sharing plan.

"While I dislike that conclusion, there seems to be no other choice. If the employees are not motivated to do quality work by the profits, then they will lose their former share of the profits. Whether or not any of us like it, the company will stop profit sharing after July 1st unless profits reach the level of the previous year.

"As long as we consider the plant as being just another company, we will not work as before. Production will not increase because our efforts will be minimal. Until we realize that, we stand the chance of losing our near ownership of 50% of the plant. We must change our attitude before it is too late. If we want to receive our share of the profits, we must act as if we are partial owners."

It would be very unusual to find six such paragraphs that contained nothing other than complex sentences because writers usually use all types of sentences. However, the sentences in those paragraphs do show how complex sentences containing adverb clauses may be used to interrelate ideas and concepts within paragraphs.

The sentences within the paragraphs also show how some complex sentences are punctuated:

1. If the adverb clause is placed at the beginning of a sentence, a comma is usually inserted after that subordinate clause (just before the independent clause).
2. If the adverb clause is placed after the independent clause and is restrictive, no comma is inserted between the independent clause and the adverb clause. (If an adverb clause is used as an afterthought, it would be unrestrictive; therefore, a comma would be placed between the independent clause and the adverb clause).

Examples of an adverb clause at the beginning of the sentence with a comma following it:

subordinating adverb
Before our meeting officially began, our boss got up and made a speech.
subject *predicate* *subject* *predicate*
subordinate clause *independent clause*

subordinating adverb
Because that speech changed most of the employees' views,
subject *predicate*
subordinate clause

I wanted to repeat it to you.
subject *predicate*
independent clause

subordinating adverb
After this plant was established
subject *predicate*
subordinate clause

the owners decided to give 50% of the profits to the employees.
subject predicate
independent clause

subordinating adverb
As long as the employees realized that,
subject predicate
subordinate clause

the profits of the plant continually increased.
subject predicate
independent clause

subordinating adverb
Although that profit sharing plan worked well during past years,
subject predicate
subordinate clause

it no longer seems to be working as well.
subject predicate
independent clause

subordinating adverb
Unless profits increase,
subject predicate
subordinate clause

the company will have to discontinue the present profit sharing plan.
subject predicate predicate
independent clause

subordinating adverb
While I dislike that conclusion,
subject predicate
subordinate clause

there seems to be no other choice.
predicate subject
independent clause

subordinating adverb

If the employees are not motivated to do quality work by the profits,

subject *predicate* *predicate*

subordinate clause

then they will lose their former share of the profits.

subject *predicate*

independent clause

subordinating adverb phrase

Whether or not any of us like it,

subject *predicate*

subordinate clause

the company will stop profit sharing after July 1st

subject *predicate*

independent clause

subordinating adverb

unless profits reach the level of the previous year.

subject *predicate*

subordinating clause

subordinating adverb phrase

As long as we consider the plant as being just another company,

subject *predicate*

subordinate clause

we will not work as before.

subject *predicate*

independent clause

subordinating adverb

Until we realize that,

subject *predicate*

subordinate clause

we stand the chance of losing our near ownership of 50% of the plant

subject *predicate* *predicate*

independent clause

subordinating
adverb
If we (want) to receive our share of the profits,
subject *predicate*
subordinate clause

subordinating
adverb phrase
we must (act) as if we (are) partial owners.
subject *predicate* *subject* *p redicate*
independent clause subordinate clause

If you will examine the preceding examples, you will find that almost every adverb clause was placed in front of the independent clause. That points to one of the main distinguishing characteristics of an adverb clause: it may be placed either before or after the independent clause. In other words, an adverb clause may be transposed to produce a transposed sentence—a sentence in which the subordinate clause comes before the independent clause.

To help the reader distinguish between the subordinate clause and the independent clause in a transposed sentence, a comma is placed between the subordinate clause and the independent clause. The comma also helps the reader quickly find the main subject of the sentence.

On the other hand, if the subordinate clause follows the independent clause, the only way to decide whether or not to use a comma is to determine whether or not the subordinate clause is restrictive or nonrestrictive. If the subordinate clause following the independent clause is restrictive, it should not be separated from the independent clause by a comma. Doing that would break up the meaning of the sentence. However, if the subordinate clause following the independent clause is nonrestrictive, there should be a comma between the independent clause and the subordinate clause.

First we will present some examples from the paragraphs of restrictive subordinate adverb clauses following independent clauses. We will also try to explain why those restrictive subordinate adverb clauses are essential to the meanings of the sentences.

Examples of restrictive subordinate adverb clauses:

adverb phrase
Whether or not any of us (like) it,
subject *predicate*
subordinate clause

the company will no longer give us 50% of the profits

subject *predicate*

independent clause

adverb

unless profits reach the level of the previous year.

subject *predicate*

subordinate clause

Please read the sentence without the last subordinate clause: "Whether or not any of us like it, the company will no longer give us 50% of the profits." That sentence has a considerably different meaning from the meaning of the example sentences. It simply states that no profits will be given to the employees. The adverb clause "unless profits reach the level of the previous year" changes the meaning of the sentence by adding a very important qualifying statement. Anytime an adverb clause adds information that changes the basic meaning of the independent clause, the adverb clause is restrictive and should not be separated from the rest of the sentence by a comma. A comma would separate essential information from the rest of the sentence, and that would be wrong.

Another example shows the same type of syntactic dependence:

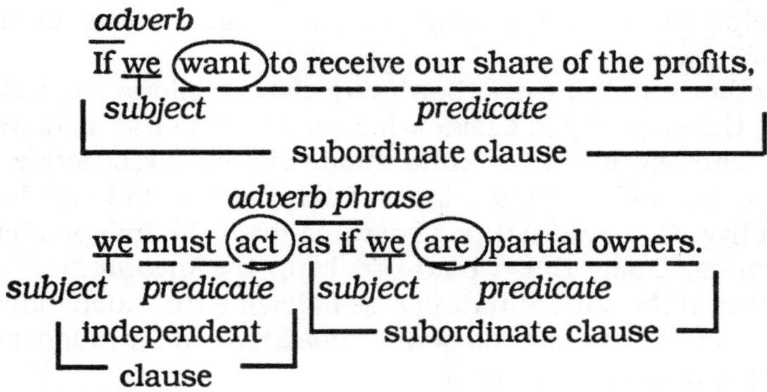

The subordinate adverb clause tells the employees how they should act, not just that they should act. "As if we are partial owners" is essential qualifying information. It implies that the employees should take a very active interest in their work and work harder. The independent clause "we must act" does not tell them how they should act so the subordinate clause following it is restrictive.

Several other sentences from the example paragraphs contain restrictive subordinate clauses following the independent clauses. Please read each sentence to see if you can discover why each subordinate adverb clause at the end of each sentence is essential to the meaning of the sentence:

No employee (had) to buy any stock in the company

subject *predicate*

independent clause

subordinating adverb

because motivation to do good work (was considered) as being

subject *predicate*

the employees' part of the investment.

predicate

subordinate clause

Men and women (spent) extra time thinking about how to do a better job

subject *predicate*

independent clause

subordinating adverb

since they (knew) they (would receive) their part of the profit.

subject *predicate* *subject* *predicate*

subordinate clause subordinate clause

•Note understood relative pronoun (they knew *that* they would receive).

introductory word

Furthermore, an employee rarely (used) all of his sick leave

subject *predicate*

independent clause

subordinating adverb

because he (wanted) to increase the profit of the plant and,

subject *predicate*

therefore, his own profit.

subordinate clause

subordinating adverb

Profit (is) down because employee production (has declined.)

subject *predicate* *subject* *predicate*

independent clause subordinate clause

subordinating adverb

Production will not increase because our efforts will be minimal.

subject *predicate* *subject* *predicate*

independent clause subordinate clause

subordinating adverb

We must change our attitude, before it is too late.

subject *predicate* *subject* *predicate*

independent clause subordinate clause

If you will recall the discussion in the paragraphs, it will be even more apparent why those subordinate adverb clauses ending the sentences were restrictive. Since the entire discussion seemed to concern increasing the profits of the plant through increasing employees' work and effort and keeping the employees' present profit sharing plan, all of the subordinate adverb clauses that ended the sentences were necessary to the entire discussion.

Not all adverb clauses ending sentences are restrictive. Many of them are nonrestrictive because they are added as afterthoughts or parenthetic information. Any time a subordinate adverb clause following an independent clause is nonrestrictive, you should use a comma to separate it from the main clause.

To see how subordinate adverb clauses can function at the ends of sentences, we will now examine some sentences containing them:

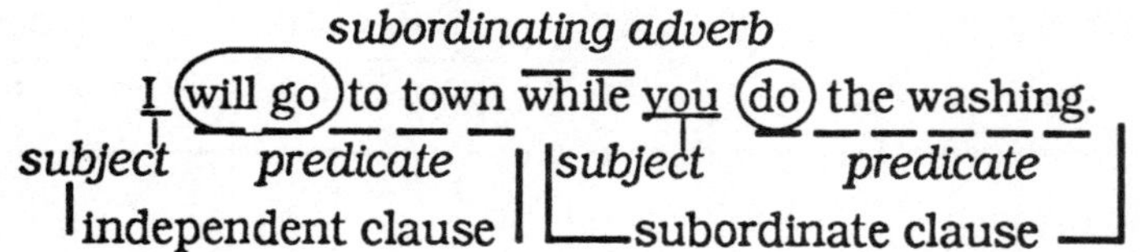

In such a sentence only a comma or the preceding discussion would tell you whether the subordinate clause was restrictive or nonrestrictive. Look at the following sentences:

subordinating adverb

When are you going to town? I will go to town while you do the washing.

subject *predicate* *subject* *predicate*

independent clause subordinate clause (restrictive)

"While you do the washing" answers the question "When are you going to town?" "While you do the washing" is restrictive in that sentence because it is used to define the time, "when", the person is going to town.

What are you going to do while I am doing the washing?

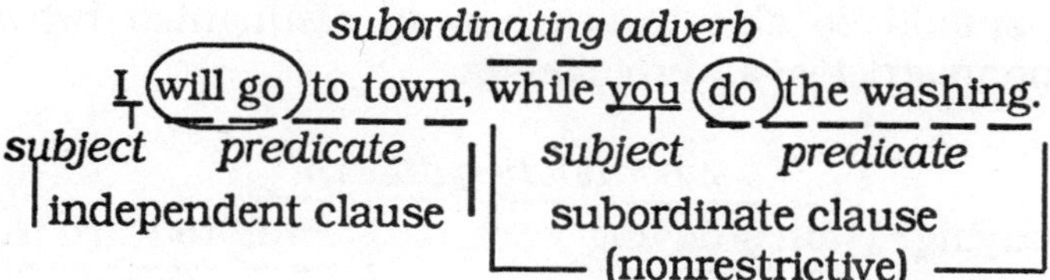

"While you do the washing" is not at all necessary to answer the question "What are you going to do while I am doing the washing?" Therefore, it is nonrestrictive and should be slightly separated from the independent clause by a comma.

Are you going to buy a new car?

I will buy a new car after Gene jumps over Niagara Falls.

If Gene is really going to jump over Niagara Falls, the adverb clause "after Gene jumps over Niagara Falls" is nonrestrictive. That adverb clause tells when the person is going to buy a new car, but the time, "after Gene jumps over Niagara Falls," is not important in answering "Are you going to buy a new car?" Therefore, "after Gene jumps over Niagara Falls" would be nonrestrictive. A comma should be used to separate that clause from the rest of the sentence:

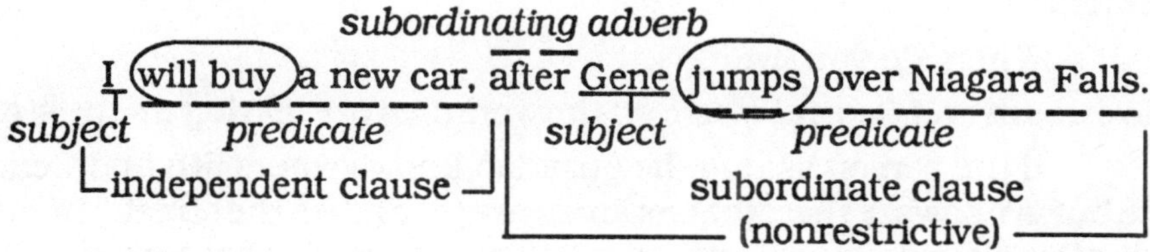

However, if the speaker answering the question was being sarcastic and using "after Gene jumps over Niagara Falls" to indicate the impossibility of his buying a car, the adverb clause would be restrictive. In other words, the meaning of the sentence would then be something similar to this: "Me buy a car? Are you crazy?" Therefore, the sentence should be punctuated like this:

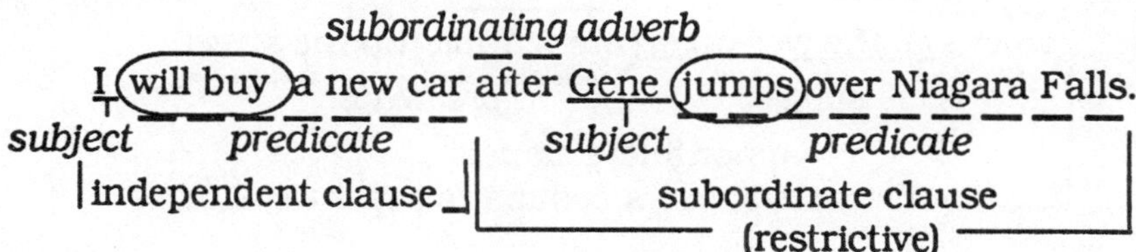

"After Gene jumps over Niagara Falls" is restrictive because it affects the entire meaning of the sentence. Therefore, no comma should be used to separate it.

Only the discussion preceding such sentences will tell you if the adverb clause is restrictive or nonrestrictive. If you will read the following sentences, you should be able to see how to distinguish between restrictive and nonrestrictive adverb clauses:

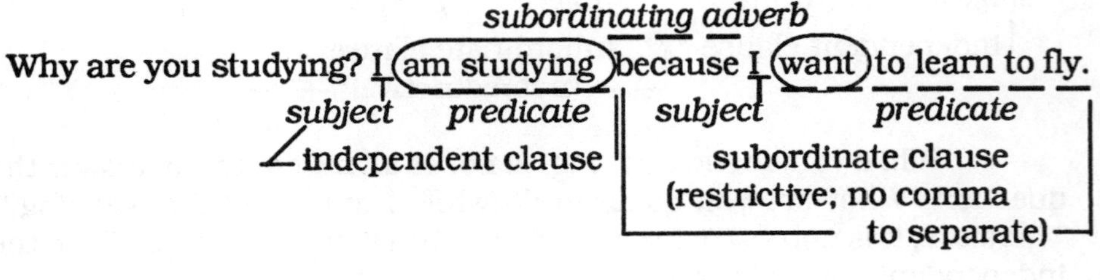

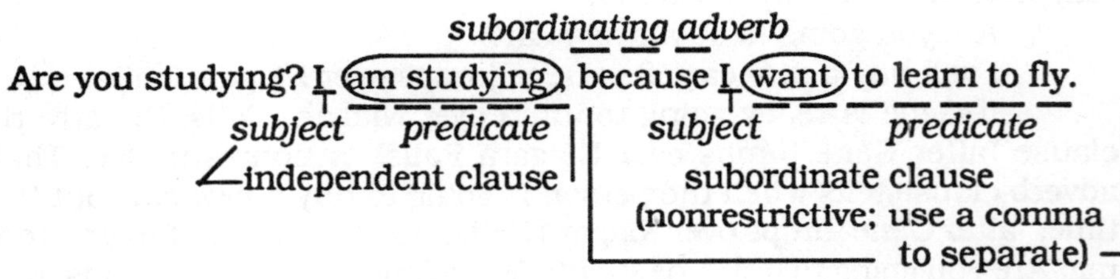

"Because I want to learn to fly" simply adds nonessential information so a comma is used to separate the adverb clause from the rest of the sentence.

Where do you live?

I live at 5th and Central where all the workmen are tearing up the street.

If the person asking the question knows where 5th and Central are but is unaware that "the workmen are tearing up the street," then the adjective clause would be nonrestrictive. It would simply add additional but unnecessary information:

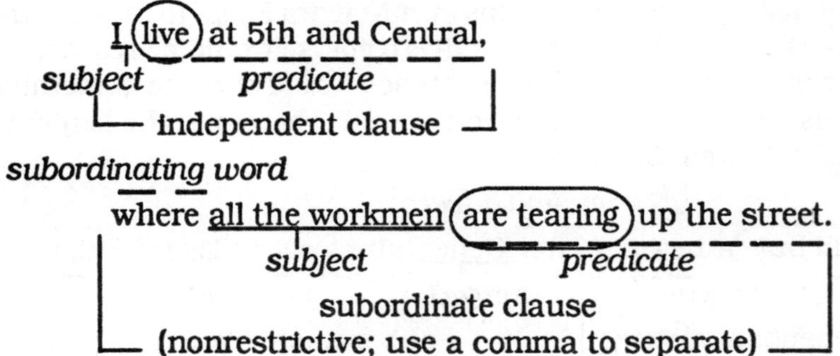

However, if the person asking the question knows "where all the workmen are tearing up the street" but is not quite sure where 5th and

Central are, the adjective clause would help the person asking the question determine where the person answering the question lives.

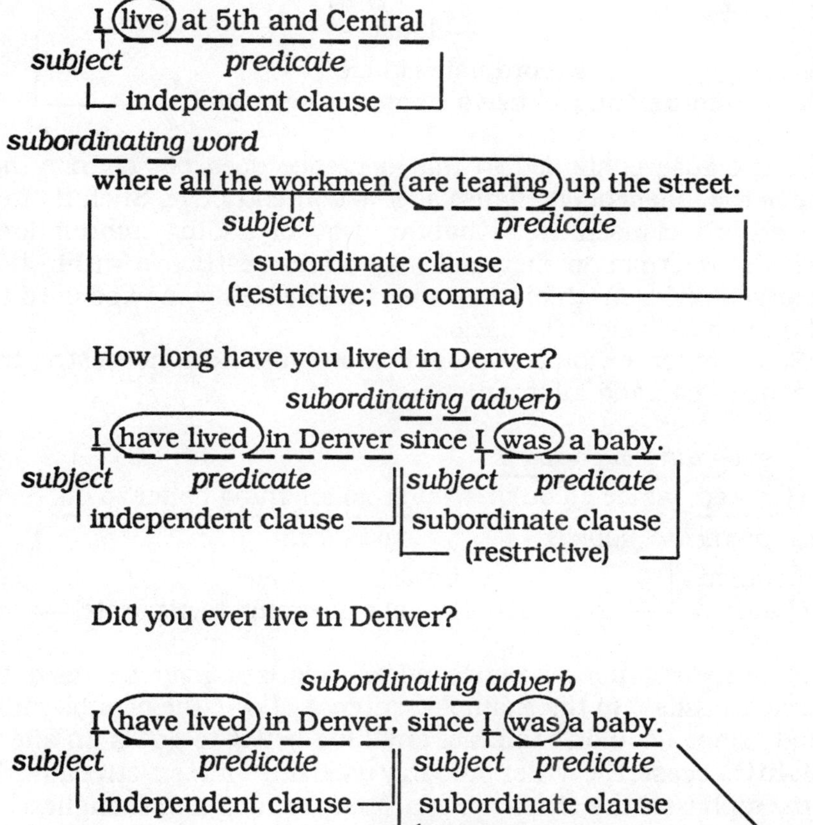

Adverb clauses are not used only when someone is answering a question. They may follow all types of sentences, and they are used regularly in paragraphs. Very often they are used to add information, although the information they add may be nonrestrictive.

The sentence that just preceded this one contained such an adverb clause:

introductory phrase

Very often they are used to add information,

subject *predicate*

independent clause

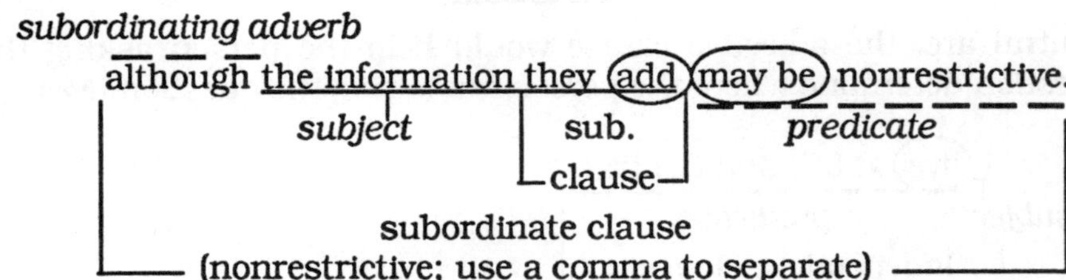

The adverb clause contained in that sentence does not change the meaning of the independent clause so it is nonrestrictive. Such nonrestrictive adverb clauses are a handy way of adding information. Although the information they add may be nonrestrictive within the particular sentences in which they are contained, they may be used to present a more thorough discussion.

Some other examples should show you how nonrestrictive adverb clauses can add information:

subordinating adverb
I moved, since I couldn't think of anything better to do.
subject predicate subject predicate
independent clause
subordinate clause
(nonrestrictive; use a comma to separate)

Commas preceding nonrestrictive adverb clauses may be used to emphasize attitudes. In the example sentence above, the comma indicates that "since I couldn't think of anything better to do" is an afterthought. In that case, the writer probably used the nonrestrictive adverb clause to emphasize the character's lack of planning and thought.

In other situations an author might use a nonrestrictive adverb clause to emphasize his own views:

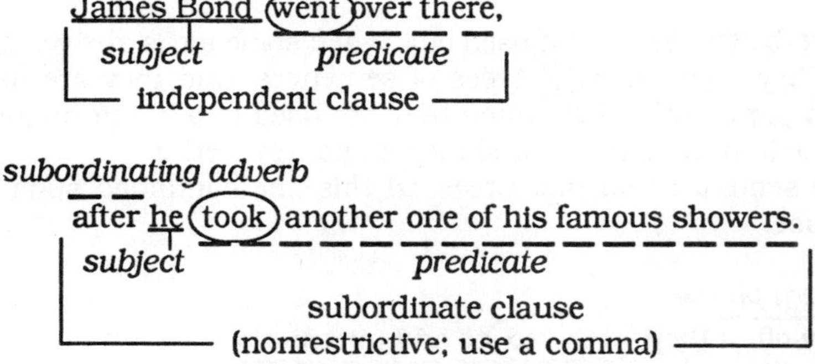

Unless something about the time "James Bond went over there" was important, the adverb clause would be nonrestrictive. If the author was being sarcastic about James Bond's taking showers all the time, such a tacked on adverb clause would be nonrestrictive and would require a comma.

Before we end this discussion of restrictive and nonrestrictive adverb clauses, we should emphasize that just because a clause, phrase, or word is nonrestrictive it does not mean that it is unnecessary to the discussion. Nonrestrictive information in a sentence is, by its very definition, unnecessary to establish the meaning of the sentence. But please remember that nonrestrictive words, phrases, and clauses may be effectively used to help develop a discussion. They may be used to add all sorts of information. They may be used to add feelings to fact. They may be used to connect ideas and information within paragraphs. They may even be used to establish connections between paragraphs.

Nonrestrictive words, phrases, and clauses can give color, life, and more meaning to your writing.

If the adverb clause is placed at the beginning of a sentence, a comma is inserted after that subordinate clause (just before the independent clause).
If the adverb clause is placed after the independent clause and is restrictive, no comma is inserted between the independent clause and the adverb clause.
If the adverb clause is placed after the independent clause and is nonrestrictive, a comma is inserted between the independent clause and the adverb clause.

SUMMARY OF MECHANICAL RULES FOR COMPLEX SENTENCES

1.If a complex sentence contains a series, separate the series with commas, just as you would in any other type of sentence.
2. If a complex sentence contains any nonrestrictive words, phrases, or clauses, use a comma or commas to separate that nonrestrictive information from the rest of the sentence.

THE COMPOUND-COMPLEX SENTENCE

Briefly, the compound-complex sentence is nothing more than a combination of a compound sentence and a complex sentence. By its very definition it must contain two independent clauses and one or more subordinate clauses. The following sentences should show you how compound-complex sentences might be constructed.

Examples:

The couch is red and the chair is purple
independent clause — *independent clause*

because those are her favorite colors.
subordinate clause

The peace treaty was signed in Paris, and the general flew home
independent clause — *independent clause*

as his wife watched the official ending of the war on T.V.
subordinate clause

As you may know, Les got into a funny argument with Bill,
subordinate clause — *independent clause*

and he insisted that Bill apologize to him in front of the entire faculty.
independent clause — *subordinate clause*

Bill told Les that no one would be stupid enough to apologize
independent clause — *subordinate clause*

to anyone over something as dumb as burning his hamburger,
continued subordinate clause

and that if Les wanted an apology
subordinate clause

he could go to the headmaster and demand one.
independent clause

After Les went to the headmaster and demanded an apology,
subordinate clause

the headmaster wrote an elaborate note to Bill,
independent clause

and he removed Bill from the job of Chief Cook and Bottle Washer.
independent clause

Although the ways of constructing compound-complex sentences are almost endless, the last example sentences should have shown you how a compound-complex sentence may tend to run on and on. If a writer is not careful, he may write what we call labyrinth sentences. Those sentences are like the mazes you see in newspapers and magazines. You can always find the beginning, but you have to trace all around to find the path to the end.

All you have to do to punctuate correctly a compound-complex sentence is use the same punctuation in it as you would use in both a compound and a complex sentence. The rules for punctuating a compound-complex sentence are the same as those for punctuating both a compound and a complex sentence. You just have to combine the rules.

SUMMARY OF MECHANICAL RULES

Apostrophe (')

The apostrophe is used for two main purposes:

1. It is used to signal ownership.
2. It is used to signal omission of letters.

Ownership or possession. Generally, when an apostrophe is used to show ownership, an apostrophe before the *s* indicates singular ownership, and an apostrophe after the *s* indicates plural ownership. It is only the nouns that have irregular plural forms that do not become possessive by adding an apostrophe after the *s*. Irregular plural noun forms are made possessive by adding apostrophe *s* ('s).

> *Place an apostrophe before the* s *to indicate that one person owns or possesses something.*

Examples of singular possession:

Lynn's	Lynn's car doesn't run.
man's	The man's hat flew into the lake.
someone's	Someone's dinner is getting cold.
one's	One's body requires food and rest.
girl's	The girl's hair is blond.
Mac's	Mac's steaks are better than yours. (Do not add an apostrophe to a personal pronoun. An apostrophe is not used to show possession with yours or its.)
chairman's	The chairman's job is very difficult.

Place an apostrophe after the s *that makes the noun plural to indicate that more than one person owns or possesses something.*

Examples of plural possession:

boys'	Boys' clothes do not always get dirtier than girls'clothes.
teachers'	The teachers' convention will be held in October.
truck drivers'	The truck drivers' favorite stop is in Gallup.
cooks'	The seven cooks' disagreement ended in a stew.
doctors'	All the doctors' offices may be found in the plaza.
Indians'	The Indians' dances are held throughout the year.

If a plural noun does not end in a s*, add apostrophe* s *('s) to that plural noun to indicate possession.*

Examples of irregular plural possession:

men's	The men's garments are found on the second floor.
women's	Women's apparel is on the first floor.
people's	People's voting habits are influenced by active politicians.
children's	The children's swimming pool is next to the adults' pool.

Omission of letters. The apostrophe is also used to indicate that one or more letters have been omitted. Contracted words—words in which letters are missing—are very common in fictional dialogue. The reason for that is obvious. To make his characters' speech sound realistic, the author uses contracted words. If you will listen to any everyday conversation, you will discover that we use contractions throughout our conversation.

Place an apostrophe wherever a letter or letters is/are missing in a contracted word.

Examples of contractions:

I'll	can't
she'll	wouldn't
he'll	didn't
I'm	it's (it is)
isn't	he's

Look at what happens if the apostrophe is left out of a contracted word.

Ill	cant
shell	wouldnt
hell	didnt
Im	its (possessive pronoun rather than contraction of *it is*)
isnt	hes

If you leave out the apostrophe, you either have an incorrectly spelled word that is harder to read, or you have a real word that means something entirely different from the same letters with an apostrophe included in the right place.

Comma

The comma is the most frequently used punctuation signal. When it is correctly used, it always provides a slight pause or separation that helps the reader.

The comma is used to provide a slight pause or separation between:

1. the greeting (salutation) and body of a non-business letter;
2. the closing and signature of a letter;
3. three or more words or noun phrases in a series;
4. two longer independent clauses in a compound sentence;
5. two short contrasting independent clauses in a compound sentence;
6. three short, parallel independent clauses with a coordinating conjunction before the last clause;
7. an introductory word, phrase, or clause and the independent clause of a sentence; any introductory element that contains a verb form should be followed by a comma;
8. the narrative and dialogue of fictional writing;
9. restrictive and nonrestrictive information in a sentence.

The comma between the greeting and the body of a letter; the comma between the closing and signature of a letter. In an informal letter a comma always follows the greeting—the greeting is the letter part where the writer might say "Dear Jane," or "Dear Uncle Dick." Some business letters also contain a comma directly following the greeting, but a colon is normally used after the salutation in a business letter.

The closing of any type of letter is always supposed to be followed by a comma. (The closing of a letter is the part where the writer writes "Love," "Sincerely," "Yours truly," "Keep it together," or some such ending before his signature.)

> *Place a comma immediately following the greeting of an informal letter.*
>
> *Place a comma immediately following the closing of a letter.*

Examples of the use of a comma following the greeting and the closing:

6400 Wyoming Blvd., N.E.
Albuquerque, New Mexico 87109
August 5, 1988

Dear Mom,

____

____

Love,

Commas between three or more words or noun phrases in a series. Anytime you have three or more words or noun phrases in a series and only one conjunction, you should place a comma after each word or phrase except the last one. The commas help the reader read the series. Although a comma before the conjunction in the series is optional, we think it is best to place a comma there too.

> *Place a comma after each word in a series except the last word, which usually follows the conjunction.*

Examples of commas between three or more words or noun phrases in a series:

Big Wally looks kind, gentle, and strong.

Our dog is light blond, dark blond, brown, and black.

The President proposed a new foreign policy, a new social policy, and a new economic policy.

Energy may be obtained from all sorts of natural sources—sunlight, natural gas, coal.

Most physical sports require intelligence, hard work, concentration, and consistent practice.

Commas between independent clauses. A compound sentence is formed when two independent clauses are joined by a coordinating conjunction. If two short and closely related independent clauses are joined by a coordinating conjunction, the comma may be omitted. However, anytime two longer independent clauses or two short contrasting independent clauses are joined by a coordinating conjunction, a comma should be placed after the word preceding the coordinating conjunction. Also, occasionally three short, parallel independent clauses will be placed together in a single sentence. When three short, parallel independent clauses are placed together in a sentence, a comma should be placed after the first clause and the second clause, again, just before the coordinating conjunction.

No comma is necessary when two short, closely related independent clauses are joined by a coordinating conjunction.

Examples of two short, closely related independent clauses that do not require a comma:

He started the fire and he cooked the steak.

She cleaned the rug and he washed the curtains.

Place a comma before the coordinating conjunction when two longer independent clauses are used to construct a compound sentence.

Examples of two longer independent clauses joined together by a coordinating conjunction:

Ralph went to the new shopping center to buy a new shirt, and he found one of the best looking shirts in town.

Janie decided to play tennis with Harriet, but Janie could not find her husband's tennis racket.

> *Place a comma before the coordinating conjunction when two short contrasting independent clauses are joined by a coordinating conjunction.*

Examples of two short contrasting independent clauses joined by a coordinating conjunction:

She wanted to laugh, but she cried instead.

The sailboat was a beauty, but the rigging broke.

> *Place a comma after the first two independent clauses when three short parallel clauses are joined in a sentence.*

Examples of three short parallel independent clauses joined together in a sentence:

He played the piano, he played the organ, and he directed the choir.

She laid out the pattern, she cut out the dress, and she made the dress.

These example sentences are actually run-on sentences and should not be used unless there is a specific reason for breaking the rules.

Commas between introductory words, phrases, or clauses and independent clauses. Most introductory words, phrases, and clauses are used for three purposes:

1. They are used for emphasizing or relating ideas contained in different sentences.
2. They are used to include nonrestrictive information.
3. They are used to transpose sentences.

If you use an introductory word, phrase, or clause for any one of those purposes, you should place a comma immediately following the word, phrase or clause (which would be just before the independent clause).

> *Place a comma between any introductory word or phrase that you want to emphasize and the independent clause following it. Introductory verbal phrases are always separated from the independent clause by a comma.*

Examples of introductory words and phrases that need commas to follow them:

Phew, working in the sewer is a drag.

Well, you don't say!

To be or not to be, that is the question.

While playing golf, he broke his wrist.

Place a comma between any introductory adverbial connective and the independent clause following it.

Examples of adverbial connectives that need commas to follow them:

However, I thought it was a good idea.

Therefore, we decided to use your plan.

Nevertheless, the payment cannot be made until we receive the product.

In fact, you might say it was a rotten idea.

(Some teachers suggest that such adverbial connectives are best used internally in sentences. In that case the adverbial connective is always nonrestrictive and should be surrounded by commas:
I, however, thought it was a good plan.)

Examples of direct addresses that need commas to follow them:

Jeff, you're a fink.

Young man, you are fired.

Jackie, can you come over?

Place a comma between an introductory verbal phrase and the independent clause following it.

Examples of introductory verbal phrases that need commas to follow them:

Lounging in the sun, she got roasted.

Trying to win, he broke his ankle.

Swimming faster and faster, he finally beat his opponent.

Any introductory verbal phrase requires a comma after it.

> *Place a comma between a long introductory prepositional phrase—which is probably a series of short prepositional phrases—and the independent clause following it.*

Examples of longer introductory prepositional phrases that need commas:

Behind the barn at the old farm house, the loveliest meadow in the world may be seen.

At 5th and 12th Streets on Saturday night, the Old Timers' Band plays.

To the right on the shelf above your head, you will find the book that you wanted.

The subordinate adverb clause is frequently placed in front of the independent clause. A sentence in which the subordinate adverb clause is placed in front of the independent clause is called a transposed sentence. When a subordinate adverb clause is placed in front of an independent clause, you should use a comma at the end of the adverb clause to create a slight separation between the subordinate adverb clause and the independent clause.

> *Place a comma between a transposed adverb clause and the independent clause following it.*

Examples of transposed adverb clauses that need commas to follow them:

If you are going to town, would you pick up some worms for our fishing trip?

When I go to town to buy the other supplies, I will also pick up some worms and salmon eggs.

After I have finished packing the trailer, I will take it down to the station.

The comma between the narrative and dialogue of fictional writing. The narrative of fictional writing is any section in which a character is not speaking. The dialogue is any section in which a character is speaking. To help the reader distinguish between the narrative and dialogue, a comma is placed between the two.

> *Place a comma between the narrative and dialogue of fictional writing if no other form of punctuation is used.*

Examples of commas between the narrative and dialogue:

He said, "I want to climb the highest mountain."

"I think I'll spend the summer in Mexico," she told him.

"Well," he said, "We'd better buy the stock now."

"Don't throw her in yet," he yelled.

A comma or commas between restrictive and nonrestrictive information in a sentence. Nonrestrictive information may be placed anywhere in a sentence; it can be placed at the beginning, in the middle, or at the end of a sentence. In fact, the mild exclamations and interjections, the adverbial connective, parenthetic words and phrases, and the direct addresses you have seen used in sentences are all nonrestrictive. They are nonrestrictive because they do not change the meanings of the sentences in which they are contained.

Nonrestrictive information is always separated from the rest of the sentence by a comma or commas. If the nonrestrictive information is placed at the beginning or the end of a sentence, only one comma is necessary to slightly separate it from the rest of the sentence. However, if the nonrestrictive information is placed in the internal part of a sentence, two commas are necessary to slightly separate the nonrestrictive information from the rest of the sentence.

> *Place a comma after any nonrestrictive information at the beginning of a sentence.*

Examples of commas following nonrestrictive information at the beginning of sentences:

Of course, he bought a new car.

No, I can't.

Well, I guess it will work.

Place a comma before and after any nonrestrictive information that is in the middle section of a sentence.

Any parenthetic statement, almost all appositives, and all direct addresses are nonrestrictive. Therefore, they should be separated from the rest of a sentence by a comma or commas. Since all appositives must follow restrictive information and most parenthetic statements follow restrictive information, we will use those in the examples.

Examples of commas before and after appositives and parenthetic statements:

John, as you know, went deep sea diving.

The chairman of the board, Jack Fisher, will become the president.

The house, which is on the corner of Quincy and Anderson, was sold.

I knew, at least I was pretty sure, that they would fly to Wyoming.

George Washington. the father of our country, never chopped down a cherry tree.

Place a comma before any nonrestrictive information that is at the end of a sentence.

Examples of commas before nonrestrictive information at the end of a sentence:

Betty is a beauty, as you could see.

I will do it soon, just as soon as I have time.

The raging sea is dangerous, of course.

You want me to clean up my room, me?

Commas used with dates, addresses, and large numbers. Commas are regularly used in materials that are not in sentence form. Although dates and addresses are often included within sentences, they are used separately more often. Written numbers from one thousand to the highest number written occur far more frequently outside a sentence structure than within sentences. However, dates, addresses, and large numbers are written using commas because commas make them easier to read.

The use of commas with dates and addresses works just as all other appositives. When the year follows the date of the month, the year is an appositive that provides more information: December 22, 1958. If that date is included within the internal part of a sentence, it must have a comma before and after the year: My daughter was born on December 22, 1958, in Denver.

> *When a date is given by itself, a comma should be placed between the date of the month and the year.*

Examples of commas in dates that are used separately:

May 24, 1985
September 25, 1963
February 27, 1951

> *When a date is included within a sentence, a comma should be placed between the date of the month and year. Another comma should follow the year if no other form of punctuation is used.*

Examples of commas in dates occurring in the middle or at the end of a sentence:

I am going to Canada on August 1, 1990.

We will make an appointment September 7, 1989.

Your letter was received on October 11, 1938, at Pampa, Texas.

I think the wreck that occurred on January 1, 1984, was caused by the snow.

Addresses usually include appositive information. The name of the state that follows the name of a city is appositive, and directions included after street names are appositive. If the street address is not included within a sentence, only a comma should be placed between the name of the street and direction: 4321 Isleta Blvd., S.W. However, if a street address is included within the internal part of a sentence and contains directions, the directions should have a comma before and after them: My friend lives at 1709 Virginia, N.E., in Albuquerque.

City and state names work the same way when they are placed together:

Flagstaff, Arizona

I teach in Flagstaff, Arizona, at the university.

If directions follow the name of a street, place a comma between the name of the street and the directions.

If the name of a state follows the name of a city, place a comma between the names of the city and state.

If the name of a street and its directions are placed in the internal part of a sentence, enclose the directions in commas.

If the name of a state immediately follows the name of a city in the internal part of a sentence, enclose the name of the state in commas.

Numbers above nine hundred ninety-nine have commas included within them to help the reader read them. What the commas actually do is set off numerical groups.

One comma is used to indicate thousands:
1,000 50,000 100,000

Two commas are used to indicate millions:
1,000,000 55,000,000 999,000,000

Three commas are used to indicate billions:
3,000,000,000 90,000,000,000 999,000,000,000

Place a comma in front of every three digits of a whole number.

Colon (:)

The colon may be used after an introduction, after the salutation in a business letter, before an example, explanation, or statement, and is consistently used to separate hours from minutes:

Salutation:
Dear Sir: Gentlemen:

Time:
10:45 a. m. 7:11 p. m. 3:30 a. m. 5:00 p. m.

Certain times are noted by the colon and period; example: "5:42.7" reads five hours, forty-two minutes, and seven seconds. Or in shorter things, like foot races, five minutes, forty-two and seven tenths seconds.

The colon following our introductory sentence shows the use of the colon following an introduction. The colons following "Salutation" and "Time" show how a colon may be used before an example.

> *Place a colon between the hours and minutes when they are written numerically.*

Dash (—)

The dash (on the typewriter, two hyphens) may be used to show interjected thoughts, sudden change in statement, definitions, and something similar to an example within a sentence.

Interjected thoughts:

The man was beating his wife—at least, I thought so.

Then I saw—could you believe it—that he was really punching at the mirror.

Sudden change in statement:

The board decided to buy stock—how dumb can a board get—although they knew its value would continue to decline.

Mary's dress was beautiful—but that's not the point.

Definitions:

A word such as *love* can be more than one part of speech—a noun or a verb.

Sociology—the study of society—is an interesting field.

Something similar to an example within a sentence:

The pool was filled with water—50,000 gallons of water.

You know how my car looks—red, white, and blue, with stars all over it—because no one can miss it.

The dash is used to indicate parenthetic information. If the parenthetic information comes at the end of a sentence, one dash is used before that parenthetic information. If the parenthetic information is placed internally in the sentence, a dash is placed before the parenthetic information, and another dash follows the parenthetic information.

Ellipsis (...)

The ellipsis indicates omission of one or more words in a quoted sentence or several words or sentences in any quotation.

Examples of ellipsis:

> He said, "The world is round. The earth rotates around the sun... and on its own axis."
>
> The critic said:
>
> > The book was nonsense...plot development was so poor that the reader could always predict what was going to happen. The characterization was so minimal that the characters were like psychological chessmen....

Place an ellipsis where any author's words are omitted in a quotation.

Exclamation Point (!)

The exclamation is the punctuation mark that is used to indicate strong emotion. If it is used following mild exclamations, it loses its emphasizing quality. Therefore, an exclamation point should only be used when you want to emphasize significantly the emotional quality of a word, phrase, or sentence.

Examine the sentences below, and you will see how an exclamation point may be properly and improperly used.

> As Matthew continued to sit at the dinner table, his mother yelled, "Get in here and help me!" (poor use unless the mother is very angry)
>
> As the woman continued to sit under the dryer, she frowned and mumbled, "I'm dying. This heat is killing me!" (poor use unless it is a truly weird hair dryer)

As Matthew watched the fire spread, he was jolted out of his trance as his buddy yelled, "Get in here and help me!"

As the woman fell over the cliff, she screamed, "I'm dying!"

Only use an exclamation point when the context is strong enough to be emphasized.

Hyphen (-)

The hyphen is used between all written numbers from twenty-one through ninety-nine. The hyphen is also used at the end of a syllable of a word that has its next syllable on another line below it. And the hyphen is used between the noun and prepositional phrase of compound words.

> *Place a hyphen between the name of the first number and the name of the second number in all numbers from twenty-one through ninety-nine.*
>
> *Place a hyphen at the end of the last syllable of a word that has its next syllable on another line below it.*
>
> *Place a hyphen or hyphens between the noun and the prepositional phrase of compound words such as sister-in-law and mother-in-law.*

Parentheses ( )

Supplementary information may be enclosed in parentheses. If you use parentheses to enclose supplementary information, you must use one parenthesis before the supplementary information and another parenthesis after the supplementary information. In other words, you must use two parentheses—one before and the other after the information.

Period (.)

The period signals the end of a declarative or imperative sentence. Since the great majority of sentences are declarative because they make some type of statement, most sentences end with a period.

The period is also used after abbreviations:

a.m.	p.m.
B.C.	A.D.
etc.	N.E.

Place a period after each letter or group of letters used in place of a word.

The period is used between whole numbers and fractions:

6.5 7.3
3.33 66.66

Place a period after the last whole number when a fraction follows it.

Place a period after a declarative or imperative sentence.

Semicolon (;)

The semicolon is used when the coordinating conjunction is omitted between two independent clauses that are joined together in a sentence. The semicolon is also used between a succession of longer phrases.

Two independent clauses joined by a coordinating conjunction:

He went to your house; he could not find you.

He looked in the park; he could not find you.

He went back home; he found you there.

Succession of longer phrases:

The artists painted cities under the ocean; sea nymphs who softly spoke to lost sailors; monster sea serpents that crushed ships to splinters; and fresh waterfalls on shore that awaited the terrified, swimming sailors.

The semicolon is also used between two sentences when one sentence is followed by another sentence beginning with an adverbial connective:

She came to the party; however, she did not stay.

They voted to sell the business; therefore, the partnership was dissolved.

Place a semicolon between two independent clauses when the coordinating conjunction is omitted.

Place semicolons between a succession of longer phrases within a sentence.

Place a semicolon between one sentence that does not end in any other form of punctuation when the next sentence begins with an adverbial connective.

Do not place a semicolon after the salutation in a letter.

Question Mark (?)

The question mark should end any sentence that requires an answer. However, some sentences may appear to be questions but actually be polite requests:

Would you please send your answer as soon as possible.

That sentence is not a question requiring an answer. It is just a polite request.

Place a question mark after any sentence that requires an answer.

Quotation Marks ("")

Quotation marks are used to enclose a character's dialogue, direct quotations, and unconventional words and phrases. When we say that a semicolon has more "pause power" than a comma, we are using "pause power" in an unconventional way. Quotation marks must be placed both before and after whatever they enclose. Otherwise, they would not enclose anything.

The most effective way to learn how to properly use quotation marks is to examine some good fictional and factual writing in which quotation marks have been used.

Place quotation marks before and after each character's dialogue, short direct quotations, and unconventional words and phrases.

Errors that Lead to Poor Reading

Probably the two most common punctuation errors are: (1) phrases or subordinate clauses that are punctuated as complete sentences; and (2) two or more sentences punctuated as one sentence. Either of these errors place an unnecessary burden on your reader so it is best to avoid such punctuation errors.

Phrases and clauses punctuated as complete sentences. Examine the following paragraph and compare it to the paragraph below it that is correctly punctuated. You will probably see why punctuating phrases and subordinate clauses as complete sentences confuses a reader.

> While Mattie went shopping. Maggie stayed home and took care of the babies. Since the babies needed a lot of her time. Maggie didn't have a chance to cook dinner. So when Mattie returned. She decided. Of course. To prepare dinner for everyone. Just as you thought.

> While Mattie went shopping, Maggie stayed home and took care of the babies. Since the babies needed a lot of her time, Maggie didn't have a chance to cook dinner. So when Mattie returned, she decided, of course, to prepare dinner for everyone—just as you thought.

(The vocabulary in the paragraphs ranged between the second and third grade levels. The syntactic level ranged between first and sixth grade levels. Therefore, if you were confused by the first incorrectly punctuated paragraph, it was the terrible punctuation that caused the confusion.)

Run-on sentences. Run-on sentences are sentences in which:

1. two independent clauses have been joined without a semicolon or a comma and a coordinating conjunction.
2. three or more independent clauses have been placed together.
   (If you will recall, you will remember that three short parallel clauses may be placed together in a single sentence. That is not the type of sentence we are referring to as a run-on sentence.)

Examine the following paragraph and compare it to the paragraph below it that is correctly punctuated. You will probably see why run-on sentences confuse a reader.

> The couple decided to buy the house they went to the bank. After they had spoken to the loan officer, they discovered that their income was not enough to qualify for a one-hundred-thousand-dollar loan they had to change their plans

> The couple decided to buy the house. They went to the bank. After they had spoken to the loan officer, they discovered that their income was not enough to qualify for a one-hundred-thousand-dollar loan. They had to change their plans.

(Again, if you were confused by the first paragraph, your confusion was not caused by the vocabulary or ideas.)

Although some people might say that you should never put more than two independent clauses together in a single sentence, you have seen that three short parallel clauses are occasionally punctuated as one sentence. There could even be a few instances when it might be helpful to run sentences together, but it is a rare time when that type of sentence is useful. Until you thoroughly understand punctuation, avoid writing run-on sentences.

The purpose of punctuation is to help the reader. If you try to put too many ideas in one sentence, you usually burden the reader. The reader may even have to go back and read your sentence again to get the meaning you wanted to convey. A run-on sentence may even confuse a reader. Those are the reasons that run-on sentences are wrong most of the time. Punctuation is not some mysterious English master who rules unwisely. Punctuation is a tool to help you get your meaning across to the reader. Punctuation errors occur when punctuation does not serve that purpose.

Broken Rules for More Meaning

Although it may seem strange to read that run-on sentences and run-on paragraphs may be useful occasionally, you may believe your eyes and mind because that is what we are to discuss. However, we are not contradicting what we have said before.

Throughout PUNCTUATION you have continually read that the purpose of punctuation is to help the reader understand the author's meaning. There are instances, particularly in fiction, when an author will ignore a punctuation rule to allow the reader to understand better the meaning of what is being read. We find run-on sentences and run-on paragraphs occasionally used by good authors to indicate rapid speech, thought, or movement. When a good author ignores punctuation rules, it is almost always to convey more meaning to the reader.

The following paragraph is quoted from "All the Years of Her Life," a short story by Morley Callaghan.* The author obviously "broke the rules" to signal rapid thought and movement.

> The mother and son walked along the street together, and the mother was taking a long, firm stride as she looked ahead with her stern face full of worry. Alfred was afraid to speak to her, he was afraid of the silence that was between them, so he only looked ahead too, for the excitement and relief were still pretty strong in him; but in a little while, going along like that in silence made him terribly aware of the strength and sternness in her; so when they were passing under the Sixth Avenue elevated and the rumble of the train seemed to break the silence, he said in his old, blustering way, "Thank God it turned out like that. I certainly won't get in a jam like that again."

In dialogue each character's speech normally should be placed in a separate paragraph. That helps the reader clearly identify the speaker and catalogue the opinions and ideas of each character. However, you may occasionally see two or more characters' dialogues placed in one paragraph. Again, the author is probably providing another signal to the reader by ignoring standard paragraphing rules. More than likely, if he is competent, the author is signaling rapid speech, an argument, confusion among the characters, or something similar that is slightly chaotic.

You may never have a reason for ignoring standard punctuation rules in your own writing. In fact, until a writer thoroughly understands punctuation, it is usually best to avoid any form of irregular punctuation. Yet, you should recognize both errors and purposely ignored rules in someone else's writing. Such recognition may help you write better, and it may even help you read with more understanding.

If you ever read something in which a good author is ignoring standard punctuation rules, pause for a moment and examine the passage. More than likely, you will understand what the author is signaling and will derive more meaning from that written page.

*"All the Years of Her Life," by Morley Callaghan. Originally published in *The New Yorker*; Copyright 1934.